Vincenzia Marais

From Pain to Purpose

A Wayfinder's Guide to Healing and Transformation

First published by Vincenzia Marais

978-1-0370-8845-2 | From Pain to Purpose | Paperback
978-1-0492-0070-5 | From Pain to Purpose | Ebook

Editor: Ellen Solomon

Proofreader: Phillipa Mitchell

Printed and bound in South Africa by Re-lease Digital
Printed and bound in all other countries by IngramSpark

Interior formatting by Gregg Davies Media
(www.greggdavies.com)

This book is also available as an e-book on all leading digital platforms

To Ruben *– my greatest teacher in love, courage, and healing*

ACKNOWLEDGEMENTS

This book is the result of many hands, hearts, and voices that supported me through its creation. I am deeply grateful to each of you:

Frans – Thank you for your consistent presence, your thoughtful reflections, and for spending countless weekends reading through chapters with me. Your companionship helped me stay grounded when I felt overwhelmed.

Ruben – You are the soul of this work. Every page is infused with what you've taught me - about resilience, about love, and about the raw beauty of showing up, even when it's hard. You are my reason and my inspiration.

Lize – For giving me the permission I didn't know I was waiting for. In moments of doubt, your encouragement gave me the courage to keep creating.

Brigitte – For planting the seed that eventually grew into this book. Your early belief in the idea helped set everything in motion.

Mom and Dad – Thank you for always being there. Your love, presence, and quiet faith have supported me in more ways than I can say.

Kerry Schmidt – Thank you for your guidance and patience as I learned how to write, and for giving me the confidence to keep going.

Ellen Solomon – Thank you for tirelessly walking beside me through the editing process with your keen eye, honesty, and unwavering commitment to helping this manuscript take shape. Your guidance sharpened my voice without ever diminishing its essence.

Phillipa Mitchell – For your patient and thorough proofreading, and for demystifying the self-publishing process. Your gentle support made a daunting journey feel possible.

Elzette Oelofse – For capturing the spirit of this book through your beautiful cover design. You brought a visual language to what lived in my heart.

Gregg Davies – Thank you for your honest feedback and your expertise in typesetting and refining my book cover. I'm also deeply grateful for the knowledge you've shared around self-publishing and for helping me strengthen my wayfinding abilities as I navigate this journey.

AI – A heartfelt thank you to the tools that supported me when my dyslexia made writing feel like a mountain. Technology helped me express what was inside me when the words felt stuck.

ABOUT THE AUTHOR

Vincenzia is a seasoned seeker, creator, life coach, and compassionate guide devoted to exploring the depth and complexity of the human journey. With years of personal healing and professional experience, she brings a heartfelt understanding of life's challenges and the transformative power that lies within each of us.

As a writer, artist, and coach, Vincenzia's work is driven by an insatiable curiosity and a deep commitment to holistic well-being. In her writing, she explores the root causes of addiction, illuminating the intricate interplay between psychology, neurobiology, spirituality, and our connection to the natural world. She honours the threads that bind us - to each other, to the Earth, and to ourselves - offering a framework for healing that is both grounded and expansive.

Her creativity finds expression in many forms: sculpting, mosaics, painting, and gardening - each one a reflection of her inner life and a practice of mindful presence. She treasures time spent with loved ones and her furry companions, whose joy and unconditional love remind her daily of what truly matters.

Above all, being Ruben's mother is the most important and meaningful part of her life. He is her greatest teacher, her compass, and the living inspiration behind her work.

Every facet of Vincenzia's life is woven into her book, From Pain to Purpose: A Wayfinder's Guide to Healing and Transformation: Navigate the Currents of Addiction and Find Your Inner Strength. With warmth, honesty, and a deep reverence for the human spirit, she invites readers to walk this path with her – to connect, to grow, and to rediscover the purpose already alive within them.

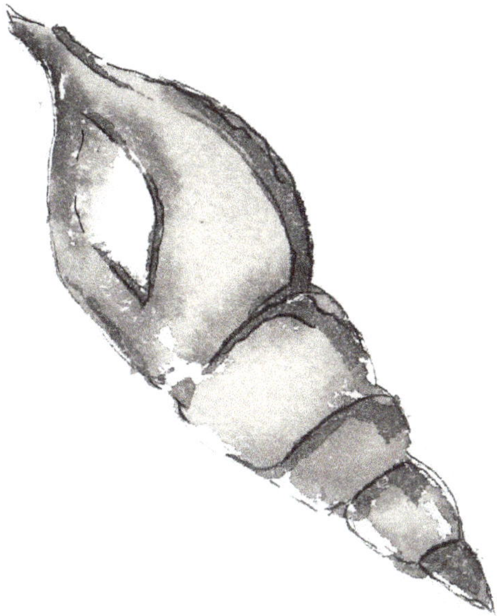

FOR MY MOTHER, VINCENZIA MARAIS SNR

Thank you for breathing life into these pages with your brush. Your Sumi-e paintings are more than illustrations; they are silent poems and soul reflections. Each stroke holds presence, patience, and a beauty that can only come from someone who listens deeply to the world within and around them.

You didn't simply create images for this book - you infused it with tenderness. What a gift it is to create beside you.

With all my love and gratitude.

If you feel drawn to the Sumi-e paintings my mother, Vincenzia Marais Snr, created for this book and would like to explore purchasing one, please feel free to contact me via email. It would be a joy to share more of her work with you.

v@karunarecovery.co.za
www.winkiemarais.co.za

CONTENTS

PREFACE II

INTRODUCTION V

The Story of the Wayfinders V
Why This Book? Why Now? VI
A Holistic and Compassionate Approach VI
An Invitation to Begin VII

SECTION 1: FOUNDATIONAL FRAMEWORK 1

CHAPTER 1 - NAVIGATING THE DEPTHS OF ADDICTION 3

A NEW PATH IN UNCHARTED WATERS 3
THE HEART OF COMPASSIONATE RECOVERY 5
The Exploration of Addiction: A Complex Tapestry 6
  Defining Addiction: A Biopsychosocial Perspective 6
  Misplaced Perspectives: Individual and Societal Addictions 7
  A Holistic Approach to Healing 8
  A Shared Journey 8
Root Causes of Addiction: A Complex Web 9
  Individual factors 9
  Social Factors 9
  Adverse Childhood Experiences (ACEs): The Deep Wounds of Early Trauma 10
  Attachment Styles and Addiction 11
  Addiction as an Attachment Condition 11
  Societal Factors 11
Addiction, Trauma, and the Role of Attachment 12
  Breaking the Cycle 12
  Healing Through Connection 13
  The Link Between Attachment Styles, Trauma, and Addiction 13
The Power of Authenticity and Attachment: Building a Fulfilling Life in Recovery 14
  Attachment Explained 14
  Authenticity Explained 14

When Connection Comes at the Cost of Authenticity 15
The Impact of Disconnection 17
Healing the Void: A Path to Authentic Living 17
Honesty and Liberation 18
The Journey Toward Authenticity and Connection 18
Chapter Takeaway 20
Unveiling the Complexity of Addiction 20
Attachment vs. Authenticity: A Delicate Balance 20
The Challenge of Balance 20
The Power of Authentic Attachment 21
Steps to Cultivate Authentic Attachment 21
Chapter 1 Summary 21
Tools and Exercises for Recovery 22
Resources for Your Journey 23

CHAPTER 2 - TRAUMA AS A CATALYST FOR ADDICTION 24

The Golden Buddha: A Tale of Hidden Treasure 24
The Definition of Trauma 25
A Case Study of Early Childhood Trauma 26
The Impact of Early Separation 26
Trauma's Footprint: Understanding Attachments, Behaviours, and Identities 27
The Path to Healing 28
The Hidden Self 28
The Unconscious Mind and Trauma 29
The Impact of Trauma on Behaviour and Identity 29
Healing from Trauma 30
Fractured Societies and Historical Trauma 30
United States: The Legacy of Slavery and Systemic Racism 31
Australia: Indigenous Peoples and Stolen Generations 31
Ireland: The Famine and Its Aftermath 31
Epigenetics: A Bridge Between Generations 32
How Does It Work? 32
Understanding Personality Patterns Through the Lens of Attachment Theory 32
Attachment Styles and Personality Patterns 33

Unpacking Maladaptive Behaviours 33
The Importance of Self-Awareness 33
Stories of Addiction and Trauma 35
Liam's Landscape: Navigating the Geography of Trauma and Addiction 35
James' Journey of Seeking Refuge 35
Addiction as a Refuge 36
The Biopsychosocial Model 36
A Story About Interconnectedness: The Biopsychosocial Analogy 36
The Biopsychosocial Model 37
Mental Health Beyond the Diagnosis: A Holistic Approach 37
Challenging the Framework: Critiques of the DSM-5 in Mental Health 38
A Call to Reframe the Narrative: Shaping a Compassionate Path to Healing 38
The Problem with Labels 39
Reclaiming Your Power: Strategies for Reframing 41
Language Shapes Perception 42
My Personal Journey with Complex Trauma: Impact, Resilience, and Healing 43
Healing Trauma and Addiction: A Journey of Mind, Body, and Spirit 44
A Holistic Approach to Well-Being 44
Culturally Sensitive and Tailored Interventions 44
Examples of Powerful Techniques 44
Expanding the Toolkit 45
A Call for a More Humane Approach to Mental Health 45
The Power of Trauma-Informed Care 45
Reclaiming Our Humanity 46
Chapter 2 Summary 48
Reflective Prompts 51
Tools and Resources 53

CHAPTER 3 - THE PLEASURE PRINCIPLE AND THE PAIN AVOIDANCE MECHANISM 57

The pursuit of pleasure and the avoidance of pain 57
Dopamine: Seeking Pleasure and Avoiding Pain 59
The Human Desire for Pleasure and 61
Aversion to Pain 61
Hijacked Highways: How Neural Pathways Fuel Addiction 66

The Problematic Reinforcement Loop 67
The Grip of Addiction 67
The Crucial Role of Dopamine in Survival: A Thought-Provoking Experiment 68
The Balancing Act: Pleasure and Pain 69
The Complex Dynamics of Addiction and Resilience 71
Understanding Cross-Addiction and Anhedonia 72
Dopamine Stacking 72
Dopamine Deluge: How Smartphones Hijack Our Brains 77
Chapter 3 Summary 80
Reflective prompts 82
Reflection Prompts for Healthcare workers, Counsellors and Coaches 83
Resources 84

CHAPTER 4 - THE HEALING POWER OF CONNECTION 86

Finding Solace in Connection 86
The Four Pillars of Recovery: A Foundation for Wholeness 89
Practical Tools for Building Your Four Pillars of Recovery 91
Beyond Isolation: The Crucial Role of Connection in Addiction Recovery 94
The Science of Connection and Addiction 94
The Transformative Power of Connection in Recovery 95
Nurturing Connection: Practical Strategies 96
Embracing the Mud: Becoming the Lotus 97
Rebuilding Wholeness: Six Core Elements of Compassionate Recovery 99
How Cognitive Distortions Create Disconnections in Addiction Recovery 101
Sobriety vs. Recovery: Understanding the Distinction 103
The Transformative Power of Recovery: Renewal and Growth 104
Chapter 4 Summary: The Healing Power of Connection 109
Reflection Prompts 113
Resources 114

CHAPTER 5 - RECLAIMING WHOLENESS 117

A Mosaic of Healing: From Shattered Pieces to a Luminous Masterpiece 117
The Road to Wholeness 118
The Wayfinding Quest of Reconnection 119
The Path to Reconnection: Letting Go and Moving Forward 120

Healing the Fractured Self: Paving the Way to Wholeness 123
Change and Wholeness Through the Lens of Neuroplasticity 124
Healing as a Collective Journey 127
Integration and Growth 127
Chapter 5 Summary 130
Resources 134

SECTION 2: DIRECT GUIDANCE FOR YOUR RECOVERY 136

CHAPTER 6 - EXPLORING FRAMEWORKS FOR COMPASSIONATE RECOVERY 137

The Adaptation of Martha Beck's Change Cycle 138
The 8 Cs of Self-Leadership 139
The 4 Cardinal Directions: A Compass for Recovery 140
The 12 Stepping Stones: A Practical Path to Healing and Wholeness 141
How to Choose the Framework That Suits Your Current Needs 141

CHAPTER 7 - THE JOURNEY INWARD: COMPASSIONATE RECOVERY AND THE POWER OF SELF-AWARENESS 147

All that glitters is not gold 147
The Power of Your Inner World 150
The Set Point and Its Influence 150
The Conductor Within: Harmonising Your Inner Orchestra 151
Discovery of the Inner Light: Spirituality as a Beacon in Compassionate Recovery 152
Walking Alongside Equals: An Egalitarian Approach to Compassionate Recovery . 165
Book recommendations 166

CHAPTER 8 - METAMORPHOSIS: EMBRACING CHANGE WITH SELF-COMPASSION 167

The Power of Change: A Familiar Friend in Disguise 168
DEATH AND REBIRTH: ENTERING THE CHRYSALIS 169
Reflection Prompts for Death and Rebirth: Entering the Chrysalis 172

DREAMING AND SCHEMING: BIRTHING POTENTIAL WITHIN THE CHRYSALIS ... 174
Reflection Prompts for Dreaming and Scheming: Birthing Potential Within the Chrysalis ... 176
THE HERO'S EMERGENCE: PREPARING TO TAKE FLIGHT ... 178
Reflection Prompts for The Hero's Emergence: Taking Flight with Renewed Strength ... 180
SOARING WITH WINGS OF TRANSFORMATION: THE PROMISED LAND ... 183
Reflection Prompts for Soaring with Wings of Transformation: The Promised Land ... 186
Resources available on Compassionate Recovery and Addiction Recovery ... 189

CHAPTER 9 - CHANNEL YOUR INNER WAYFINDER: THE 8 CS OF SELF - LEADERSHIP ... 190

Crisis Cultivates Opportunity ... 190
The 8 Cs of Self-Leadership ... 192

CHAPTER 10 - THE CARDINAL DIRECTIONS OF COMPASSIONATE RECOVERY: NAVIGATING THE STORM ... 201

From Gridlock to Growth ... 201
Navigating the Storm ... 206
The 4 Cardinal Directions: Planning Your Recovery Journey ... 209
The 1st Cardinal Direction – Response-Ability: The Foundation of Empowerment ... 209
The 2nd Cardinal Direction – Acceptance: The Path to Understanding ... 216
The 3rd Cardinal Direction – Forgiveness: The Key to Healing ... 226
The 4th Cardinal Direction Hope – The Beacon Illuminating the Path ... 233
How the Four Cardinal Directions Support Healing: Interconnectedness and Synergy 238
Resources ... 241
Conclusion ... 242

PREFACE

"This being human is a guest house.

Every morning a new arrival.

A joy, a depression, a meanness,

Some momentary awareness comes

As an unexpected visitor.

Welcome and entertain them all!

Even if they're a crowd of sorrows,

Who violently sweep your house

Empty of its furniture,

Still, treat each guest honourably.

He may be clearing you out

For some new delight.

The dark thought, the shame, the malice,

Meet them at the door laughing,

And invite them in.

Be grateful for whoever comes,

Because each has been sent

As a guide from beyond."

– Rumi

We have all felt it – the sharp sting of loss, the dull ache of disappointment, or the overwhelming weight of trauma. Pain, in all its forms, is an inescapable part of being human. While it can feel consuming, it also carries with it the potential for transformation. In pain lies a message – a guide urging us to explore the depths of who we are and who we might become.

Yet, instead of embracing the lessons pain can teach us, many of us retreat into distraction or denial. We may numb our emotions with screen time, substances, or compulsive behaviours, mistaking avoidance for relief. But healing begins not in escape but in turning inward – with curiosity and courage – to face our discomfort and listen to its wisdom.

This book was born out of the understanding that pain, when met with compassion and intention, can become a catalyst for profound growth. Rather than something to flee from, it becomes a teacher, reshaping the way we see ourselves and the world.

An Invitation to Transformation

This journey focuses on wholeness rather than perfection. It integrates pain, creating space for light to enter and inspires growth. The chapters ahead will serve as a companion through this process, offering insights, tools, and stories to help you navigate your own transformation.

Rumi's poem reminds us that every experience, no matter how difficult, is an invitation to grow. It calls us to welcome all aspects of our humanity, trusting that even our darkest moments carry the potential for inner change.

As you embark on this journey, know that you are not alone. Your pain has meaning, your resilience has power, and your story is still unfolding. Let this book guide you toward discovering the strength and purpose that lie within.

Welcome to the beginning of your transformation. Let us take the first step together.

INTRODUCTION

We are all Wayfinders on the vast and unpredictable ocean of life. Much like the Polynesian navigators who charted their journeys across uncharted waters, we, too, are tasked with steering through the challenges that shape our existence. The storms of pain – loss, trauma, addiction – can leave us adrift, unsure of our direction. Yet, these storms, as unwelcome as they may seem, hold within them the seeds of transformation.

Pain is a universal experience, but our response to it is uniquely our own. While many of us seek refuge in distraction or denial, true healing begins when we choose to face our suffering with courage and curiosity. This book is an invitation to embark on a significant journey – one where pain is not the end but the beginning of something greater. It offers a way to turn adversity into strength, transform suffering into purpose, and navigate the depths of your inner world with compassion and resilience.

THE STORY OF THE WAYFINDERS

Imagine a vast ocean beneath a starlit sky, where Polynesian Wayfinders navigated their journeys across the Pacific without maps or instruments. These remarkable navigators relied on their deep connection to the natural world, interpreting the patterns of stars and the rhythm of waves. For example, the way the waves broke against their boat was a vital source of information. Each wave's height, frequency, and direction provided information about underwater formations, currents, and nearby landmasses. With every crest and trough, they could infer the presence of reefs, the flow of tides, and even potential threats, guiding them safely on their voyages across the vast and mysterious ocean.

The Wayfinders embraced uncertainty, venturing into the unknown with courage and ingenuity. They did not fear the horizon; they revered it as a mystery filled with possibility. The ocean became a mirror of their spirit: expansive, adaptable, and profoundly resilient.

For the Wayfinders, navigation was much more than reaching a destination; it was forging a path through uncharted waters. They trusted in their ability to read the signs around them and within themselves. Their perseverance created life and culture across countless islands.

Their incredible skills and abilities were so profound that many at the time believed they were a type of shaman, capable of performing magic. Recovery mirrors their journey. It is a voyage into the unknown, requiring courage, adaptability, and an openness to transform. The wisdom of the Wayfinders reminds us that the journey encompasses more than just where we are going; it also includes who we become along the way. Their legacy serves as a testament to humanity's innate ability to adapt, persevere, and thrive in the face of uncertainty. Like the Wayfinders, we, too, are capable of navigating life's challenges with courage, grace and resilience.

WHY THIS BOOK? WHY NOW?

In a fast-paced world overflowing with distractions, it has become easier than ever to avoid the discomfort of pain. We swipe, scroll, shop, and seek substances to escape the feelings we'd rather not face. But avoidance comes at a cost. It keeps us tethered to our suffering, bound by the very chains we seek to escape.

This book offers an alternative. Grounded in ancient wisdom and modern science, it provides a holistic framework for navigating pain and discovering purpose. Drawing from psychology, neurobiology, philosophy, and spirituality, From Pain to Purpose combines insights with practical tools to help you transform your life.

A HOLISTIC AND COMPASSIONATE APPROACH

Recovery is a nonlinear path and an ever-evolving process. This book recognises that healing requires addressing every dimension of being – mind, body, and spirit. Whether you are grappling with addiction, loss or a longing for purpose, the tools and stories within these pages will resonate with your experience.

You will find strategies rooted in mindfulness, self-compassion, and trauma-informed care, along with reflections inspired by cultural and spiritual wisdom. Together, these elements create a holistic approach to healing that is both practical and profound.

AN INVITATION TO BEGIN

Rumi's words resonate with the essence of this journey: "Be grateful for whoever comes, because each has been sent as a guide from beyond."

Every challenge, every moment of despair, every flicker of hope is a visitor to be welcomed. Each carries a lesson, a gift, or a chance for transformation.

As you turn the pages of this book, may you feel a sense of companionship on your journey. You are not alone in your pain, and you are not alone in your healing. Together, let us navigate the currents of life, transforming pain into purpose and discovering the resilience that lies within us all.

This is your odyssey. The first step is yours to take. Let's begin.

SECTION 1: FOUNDATIONAL FRAMEWORK

Welcome to the first section of From Pain to Purpose. In this foundational framework, I lay the groundwork for your compassionate recovery journey by introducing the key concepts and essential context you need to understand the process of healing. This section provides a comprehensive overview of the challenges faced and the transformative potential that lies within each experience. By exploring the roots of pain and the early steps toward recovery, you will gain clarity on the tools and perspectives necessary for growth.

This framework sets the stage for the personalised guidance to follow, equipping you with a solid base from which to build a meaningful and lasting transformation.

CHAPTER 1 - NAVIGATING THE DEPTHS OF ADDICTION

A NEW PATH IN UNCHARTED WATERS

Recovery, like life, is far from a straight line. It is not a one-size-fits-all journey but an intricate dance of progress, setbacks, and resilience. Healing from addiction, trauma, or loss is as much about uncovering the roots of suffering as it is about reclaiming the authentic self. It requires not only overcoming dependence but also rediscovering the parts of yourself that have been obscured by pain.

This process is neither predictable nor easy. It often feels like navigating uncharted waters, where familiar maps fail, and the destination remains unclear. Yet, it is in this uncertainty that the most meaningful growth occurs. The story of Sarah, like so many others, illustrates this truth – a journey of despair, courage, and transformation.

Sarah's Story

Sarah stares at the faded map on her kitchen table, the crimson line mocking her relentless pursuit of recovery. Years of trying – and failing – to break free from addiction erode her self-belief, leaving her adrift in a sea of despair. The fear of relapse is a gnawing presence, constantly threatening to pull her under. She longs for a life of joy, purpose, and connection, but the path forward feels obscured and tangled in uncertainty.

The map bears the scars of her struggle: coffee stains, frayed edges, and countless revisions. A bold inscription in glaring red ink declares her recovery – a finality that feels like a cruel taunt. With frustration boiling over, she slams her fist on the table, the sound echoing in her empty apartment.

Yet, even in her despair, a flicker of hope stirs – a yearning to reclaim her future, no matter how daunting the journey. Her eyes fall upon a sticky note, its sunrise-orange hue a striking contrast to the dull steel of the fridge.

"Be here now. Seek wisdom, not certainty."

The words pierce through the fog that clouds her mind. Sarah realises that her relentless pursuit of certainty is her downfall. She believes recovery, like life, must follow a linear, predictable path. But the note's wisdom beckons her to embrace the unknown – to venture into the untamed terrain where true growth flourishes.

With trembling hands, Sarah picks up a pen. Her first act of defiance against the darkness is small but significant: bookmarking a mindfulness class on her phone and circling a date on the calendar. It is a humble beginning, but it is enough to shift something within her.

A Compass Within

The journey has its challenges. Days of self-doubt creep in, and the allure of old habits threatens to pull Sarah back. But she discovers a powerful truth: she doesn't need to rely on the rigid lines of an external map. Instead, she can navigate by the internal compass of her mind and heart.

Sarah's realisation mirrors a truth deeply rooted in many cultures: the interconnectedness of mind and heart. She embraces mindfulness as her path to healing, cultivating awareness, intuition, self-compassion, and resilience. Each small act of mindfulness becomes a stepping stone, helping her transform obstacles into opportunities.

A Way Forward

Sarah's story is profoundly human. Like so many others, she finds that the path to recovery does not involve following perfect steps but instead is more about being present. It is less about creating certainty and more about learning to dance with the unknown. Her journey reminds us that healing is possible – not through preconceived, one-size-fits-all rigid plans, but through a willingness to show up, be open and embrace the unfolding process.

The journey of recovery is daunting but transformative. It teaches us not only how to navigate the uncharted waters of pain but also how to rediscover the strength, wisdom, and light that reside within. Sarah's story is your story – an invitation to chart your own path, guided not by external maps but by the compass of your own heart and mind.

THE HEART OF COMPASSIONATE RECOVERY

Compassionate Recovery (CR) offers a holistic, mindful, and trauma-informed approach to healing. It acknowledges that recovery is deeply personal and multifaceted, involving physical, emotional, and spiritual dimensions. CR prioritises wisdom over certainty by encouraging you to explore your unique path with patience and self-compassion.

Addiction is complex, with visible and hidden challenges woven into its fabric. CR helps you address these layers by promoting self-awareness and resilience. It provides the tools to navigate the uncertainties of recovery while nurturing deeper connections with yourself and others.

Sarah's story exemplifies the essence of CR. Her journey wasn't perfect or linear – it was dynamic, filled with setbacks and triumphs. Yet, through compassion and perseverance, she found a way to reclaim her life.

This path is not focused on achieving perfection but instead on progress. It's focused on uncovering the inner strength to face the uncharted waters of addiction and discovering the boundless possibilities that lie beyond. CR invites us all to embark on this journey of self-discovery and healing, reminding us that even in uncertainty, there is beauty and hope.

Embark on Your Journey

Like a Wayfinder, you are empowered to navigate the turbulent seas of addiction and chart a course toward healing and wholeness. With courage, resilience, and a willingness to learn, you can transform pain into purpose.

Are you ready to start your journey?

THE EXPLORATION OF ADDICTION: A COMPLEX TAPESTRY

Addiction is a multifaceted condition that defies simplistic explanations. It is not a matter of moral weakness or a lack of willpower but rather a persistent brain condition characterised by compulsive engagement in rewarding behaviours, even when those behaviours result in harm. This destructive cycle overwhelms the ability to abstain, regardless of the negative consequences.

While substance abuse is a common form of addiction, it is crucial to recognise that addiction can manifest in many other ways. Gambling, disordered eating, excessive internet use, online gaming, and even extreme people-pleasing can become compulsive and harmful. These behavioural addictions can wreak havoc on relationships, careers, and overall well-being, leading to outcomes similar to substance dependence.

The mechanisms driving addiction are remarkably consistent across its many forms. They stem from a complex interplay of biological, psychological, social, and environmental factors. These layers intertwine to form a tapestry of influences that shape the development and progression of addiction.

By exploring the brain's reward system, the role of environmental cues, and the psychological factors that sustain these patterns, we can begin to unravel the complexity of addiction. This deeper understanding is essential for promoting effective recovery and long-term resilience.

Defining Addiction: A Biopsychosocial Perspective

Addiction is best understood through a biopsychosocial lens, which accounts for the intricate interactions of biological, psychological, and social factors. It is not merely a chemical dependency or a personal failing but a learned behaviour shaped by multiple influences.

At the biological level, addiction rewires the brain's reward system. Engaging in addictive behaviours or substances triggers the release of dopamine, a neurotransmitter associated with pleasure and motivation. Over time, repeated exposure to these stimuli alters the brain's circuitry, reducing the ability to feel pleasure from everyday experiences and making cravings almost impossible to resist.

Psychologically, factors such as trauma, chronic stress, depression, and anxiety play a significant role. Addiction often serves as an attempt to self-soothe or escape from emotional pain. These behaviours become entrenched as coping mechanisms, creating a vicious cycle that reinforces dependency.

Socially, addiction is shaped by family dynamics, cultural norms, and societal pressures. Peer influence, familial addiction history, and systemic issues such as poverty or limited access to healthcare can significantly increase vulnerability to addictive behaviours.

Understanding addiction as a learned behaviour helps challenge stigmas that label it a moral failing. It emphasises that addiction is a response to internal and external pressures rather than a character flaw, creating space for compassion and constructive solutions.

Misplaced Perspectives: Individual and Societal Addictions

Society often holds a contradictory view of addiction, celebrating ambition, drive, and consumption while condemning substance abuse. This duality obscures the shared essence of these compulsions: both are driven by an inability to stop seeking more, regardless of the cost.

Addiction manifests on a societal level in our relentless pursuit of power, wealth, and consumption. These behaviours, while often glorified, mirror the compulsive patterns of substance addiction. The consequences are equally dire, leading to environmental degradation, widening inequalities, and climate change.

Just as addiction to substances takes a toll on individuals, societal addiction has far-reaching consequences. Our collective dependence on growth and material wealth not only harms the planet but also perpetuates systems of exploitation and unsustainable living. Addressing addiction at this level requires challenging the underlying economic, political, and social structures that drive these patterns.

A Holistic Approach to Healing

Whether individual or societal, addressing addiction requires a holistic approach. This means recognising its multifaceted nature and addressing the biological, psychological, social, and environmental factors that contribute to it. On an individual level, this may involve therapies that promote self-awareness, coping skills, and emotional resilience. On a societal level, it calls for systemic change – rethinking economic models, prioritising sustainability, and promoting equity.

The path to overcoming addiction requires a revelatory shift in consciousness. At its core, this shift involves cultivating empathy, understanding, and interconnectedness. By nurturing a culture of compassion, cooperation, and sustainability, we can create conditions for both personal and collective healing.

A Shared Journey

Addiction, in all its forms, highlights the need to find relief or to feel connected. Recognising this shared experience reminds us that the journey of recovery is not one of isolation but of collaboration and mutual growth.

In facing the complexities of addiction, whether in ourselves or in the surrounding systems, we take the first steps toward meaningful transformation. Through holistic understanding, intentional action, and a commitment to empathy, we can navigate these uncharted waters and move closer to a future defined by healing, sustainability, and hope.

ROOT CAUSES OF ADDICTION: A COMPLEX WEB

Understanding addiction requires delving into the interplay of individual, societal, and environmental factors. These elements combine to create a complex tapestry that shapes addiction's development and perpetuation. By examining these roots, we gain insight into the dynamics that drive addiction and inform strategies for recovery.

Individual factors

Biological Factors

- **Genetic predispositions**: Certain genetic traits can increase vulnerability to addiction, affecting brain chemistry and reward pathways.
- **Brain chemistry and structure**: Neurobiological changes, particularly in the brain's reward and impulse control centres, play a central role in addiction.

Psychological Factors

- **Mental health conditions**: Disorders such as depression, anxiety, or bipolar disorder often intersect with addiction, creating cycles of dependency as individuals seek relief.
- **Personality traits**: Characteristics like impulsivity and sensation-seeking can predispose individuals to addictive behaviours.
- **Coping mechanisms**: Addiction frequently develops as a maladaptive strategy for managing emotional pain, trauma, or stress.

Social Factors

- **Peer pressure**: Social dynamics can encourage or normalise addictive behaviours, particularly in youth.

- **Family history**: A legacy of addiction within families often influences susceptibility.
- **Social isolation**: A lack of meaningful connections or support can exacerbate addiction risk.

Adverse Childhood Experiences (ACEs): The Deep Wounds of Early Trauma

ACEs are traumatic events that occur during childhood, such as abuse, neglect, or household dysfunction. They are among the most significant predictors of addiction and mental health challenges.

The Connection Between ACEs and Addiction

ACEs disrupt healthy brain development, impairing emotional regulation and coping mechanisms. Individuals with a history of ACEs are more likely to turn to addictive behaviours as a way to numb pain or navigate overwhelming emotions.

Other Forms of Childhood Trauma

Beyond traditional ACEs, additional factors can leave lasting scars:

- **Parental dismissal or invalidation**: Creates feelings of worthlessness and isolation.
- **Criticism or neglect**: Erodes self-esteem and promotes insecurity.
- **Parental conflict or abandonment**: Leaves children struggling with trust and stability.
- **Unrealistic expectations and comparisons**: Fuel anxiety, stress, and low self-worth.

Understanding the impact of ACEs allows for targeted prevention and treatment strategies, addressing the roots of addiction rather than its symptoms.

Attachment Styles and Addiction

Attachment styles, shaped during childhood, influence how we form relationships and manage stress:

- **Secure**: Trusting, emotionally balanced, and able to maintain healthy relationships.
- **Anxious-Preoccupied**: Crave intimacy but fear abandonment, leading to clingy behaviour.
- **Avoidant-Dismissive**: Value independence and avoid emotional vulnerability.
- **Fearful-Avoidant**: Desire closeness but fear rejection, creating mixed signals in relationships.

Addiction as an Attachment Condition

Addiction often emerges as a substitute for unmet attachment needs. When secure bonds are lacking, substances or behaviours may serve as temporary relief or connection. This perspective highlights the importance of nurturing authentic relationships in recovery, as the opposite of addiction is typically said to be connection.

Societal Factors

Economic Influences

- **Poverty and inequality**: Economic hardship exacerbates stress and limits access to resources.
- **Unemployment**: This can lead to a loss of identity and increased vulnerability to addictive behaviours.

Social Influences

- **Discrimination and exclusion**: Marginalisation contributes to emotional pain and isolation.
- **Healthcare disparities**: Limited access to mental health services perpetuates cycles of addiction.
- **Media influence**: Glamorisation of substance use or behaviours can normalise addiction.

Environmental Factors

- **Substance availability**: Easy access increases the likelihood of abuse.
- **Community norms**: Cultural attitudes toward addiction shape its prevalence and stigma.
- **Policy and politics**: Systems that prioritise punishment over rehabilitation often fail to address the root causes of addiction.

ADDICTION, TRAUMA, AND THE ROLE OF ATTACHMENT

Addiction and trauma often exist in a mutually reinforcing cycle. Trauma disrupts healthy attachment patterns, leaving us vulnerable to addiction as a coping mechanism. At the same time, addiction perpetuates disconnection, reinforcing feelings of isolation and unworthiness.

Breaking the Cycle

Understanding the link between attachment and addiction is crucial for recovery:

- Building self-awareness about attachment patterns can help us identify relational triggers.

- Developing healthier coping strategies promotes emotional regulation and resilience.
- Strengthening genuine connections replaces the false comfort of addiction with authentic fulfilment.

Healing Through Connection

Recovery is about restoring connections – with oneself, others, and the world. By addressing the roots of addiction and fostering secure attachment, we can replace cycles of disconnection with growth and meaningful relationships.

This holistic approach, much like the Wayfinders navigating their journeys, empowers us to respond to emotional challenges with intention and resilience, charting a course toward lasting recovery and genuine fulfilment.

The Link Between Attachment Styles, Trauma, and Addiction

Attachment styles formed during childhood profoundly shape how we navigate trauma and relationships in adulthood. Secure attachment provides a foundation of trust and stability, enabling healthy coping mechanisms. In contrast, insecure attachment, whether anxious, avoidant, or disorganised, leaves us more vulnerable to trauma's effects, including addiction.

Addiction complicates these dynamics further. It disrupts healthy attachment patterns, perpetuates cycles of disconnection, and reinforces maladaptive coping mechanisms. Substances or behaviours often become substitutes for genuine connection, numbing emotional pain or providing a fleeting sense of comfort.

Healing requires addressing both addiction and attachment-related challenges. By promoting secure connections with oneself and others, we can replace the false solace of addiction with the genuine fulfilment of authentic relationships. This dual approach lays the groundwork for lasting recovery and emotional well-being.

THE POWER OF AUTHENTICITY AND ATTACHMENT: BUILDING A FULFILLING LIFE IN RECOVERY

Dr Gabor Maté, a leading expert in addiction and trauma, emphasises that authenticity and attachment are fundamental to human survival and well-being. Attachment reflects our need for emotional connection and security, while authenticity is the ability to live in alignment with our true selves. These two forces, when balanced, enable deep, meaningful connections and personal growth.

Attachment Explained

Attachment plays a vital role in early development and lifelong well-being. At birth, endorphins released by both mother and baby foster a bond essential for survival. This secure attachment supports the development of the prefrontal cortex (PFC), which governs:

- Emotional regulation: Managing and modulating emotions.
- Impulse control: Inhibiting rash decisions and prioritising long-term goals.
- Executive functioning: Facilitating problem-solving, reasoning, and adaptability.

The PFC matures slowly, reaching full development in early adulthood, making secure attachments crucial for navigating life's challenges.

Authenticity Explained

Authenticity involves being true to yourself – expressing your genuine feelings, thoughts, and identity. In early human history, authenticity ensured survival by enabling self-trust. In modern contexts, authenticity allows us to align our lives with our values, creating personal fulfilment.

Secure attachments foster authenticity by providing emotional safety, enabling us to express our true selves. Conversely, when attachments feel threatened, authenticity may be suppressed to maintain relational security.

When Connection Comes at the Cost of Authenticity

Sandy's Story

Sandy grew up in a volatile household marked by unpredictability and explosive rage. To survive, she suppressed her true feelings, avoided conflict, and accommodated others' needs, sacrificing her authenticity to preserve a fragile sense of safety.

As an adult, Sandy struggled with internal conflict and low self-worth. Despite professional success, she felt powerless and disconnected. Her childhood conditioning had taught her that safety required self-denial, leaving her yearning for authenticity while fearing the consequences of expressing her true self.

Through coaching and self-reflection, Sandy began to confront the past and reclaim her authentic identity. Her journey highlights the tension between connection and authenticity and the transformative potential of self-awareness, compassion, and courage.

Sandy's story serves as a compelling case study of the enduring impact of childhood experiences on adult identity and emotional well-being. It reveals several interconnected themes that illustrate the journey from trauma to healing:

Impact of a Chaotic Upbringing: Sandy's upbringing in a volatile household highlights how instability and emotional turbulence can deeply impact someone's ability to express and understand their feelings. This environment promotes survival tactics, such as the suppression of true emotions and avoidance of conflict – common responses to preserve a semblance of safety in chaotic circumstances.

Sacrifice of Authenticity: The cost of Sandy's coping strategies becomes evident as she sacrifices her authenticity for the sake of safety. This theme highlights a common dilemma faced by many people from dysfunctional families – choosing between self-expression and the need for security. It illustrates how early experiences can lead to internalised beliefs that one's worth is tied to pleasing others, often at the expense of one's identity.

The Paradox of Success: Despite achieving professional success, Sandy feels powerless and disconnected, reflecting a dissonance between external accomplishments and internal fulfilment. This paradox highlights the idea that success does not equate to happiness or self-worth. Her story reminds us that personal fulfilment arises not from societal measures of success but from alignment with one's true self.

The Journey Toward Healing: Sandy's path of self-reflection and coaching illustrates the possibility of healing and reclaiming one's identity. This transformative journey emphasises that confronting past traumas is essential for personal growth. It also indicates that seeking help, whether through coaching or therapy, can be a pivotal step in rediscovering authenticity.

Connection vs. Authenticity: The tension between connection and authenticity is a powerful theme throughout Sandy's story. Her struggles reveal a universal truth: the desire for connection is often accompanied by the fear of vulnerability. This dichotomy can make it challenging for people to form genuine relationships because they grapple with the fear of rejection or judgment when expressing their true selves.

Power of Self-Awareness and Compassion: Ultimately, Sandy's story conveys a message of hope and resilience. Through the development of self-awareness and self-compassion, people can navigate the complexities of their identities and begin to embrace their authentic selves. The narrative demonstrates that healing is a process - one that requires courage and a willingness to confront uncomfortable truths.

The Impact of Disconnection

When we suppress our authentic selves to prioritise connection, the consequences can be far-reaching:

- **Emotional distress**: Feelings of emptiness, isolation, and dissatisfaction.
- **Relationship difficulties**: Struggles with intimacy, trust, and vulnerability.
- **Low self-esteem**: A diminished sense of self-worth and self-acceptance.
- **Mental health challenges**: Increased risk of anxiety, depression, and maladaptive coping behaviours.
- **Physical health issues**: Chronic stress, pain, and autoimmune conditions.

These patterns often perpetuate cycles of addiction as we turn to substances or behaviours to fill the void left by disconnection.

Healing the Void: A Path to Authentic Living

Healing begins with understanding the roots of our disconnection and embracing the process of self-compassion. Pioneering psychologists like John Bowlby and Mary Ainsworth have shown that secure attachment nurtures emotional resilience and healthy interpersonal skills. Similarly, self-determination theory emphasises the importance of autonomy, relatedness, and competence in fostering well-being.

By reconnecting with your authentic self and nurturing secure relationships, you can move beyond the cycle of external validation and discover the fulfilment that comes from within.

Honesty and Liberation

Healing requires emotional honesty. Much like the Wayfinders, who assessed their vessels and surroundings with unflinching accuracy, we must confront the truths we avoid. Denial may feel protective in the moment, but it ultimately perpetuates cycles of suffering. True liberation begins when we courageously acknowledge our reality and take steps to address it.

This process is not about assigning blame but raising understanding and emotional honesty. By embracing authenticity, we open the door to healing, connection, and growth.

The Journey Toward Authenticity and Connection

Recovery and personal growth are about reclaiming authenticity and fostering meaningful relationships. This journey involves:

1. **Acknowledging past wounds**: Recognising the ways disconnection has shaped your life.
2. **Cultivating self-compassion**: Treating yourself with kindness and understanding.
3. **Building secure attachments**: Forming connections based on trust and emotional safety.
4. **Embracing vulnerability**: Allowing yourself to be seen and known as you truly are.

By addressing the root causes of disconnection and cultivating self-compassion, you can break free from the cycle of seeking external validation. True fulfilment comes not from external achievements but from aligning with your authentic self and promoting genuine connections.

This journey is ongoing, and every step brings you closer to a life of empowerment, purpose, and inner peace. With courage and commitment, you can reclaim your life, heal past wounds, and build a future defined by authenticity and meaningful connection.

MY INVITATION TO YOU

Dear Fellow Traveller,

The journey of addiction recovery is far more than the act of abstaining from harmful substances or behaviours – it is an exploration of your true self. Addiction often serves as a shield, masking our vulnerabilities and protecting us from rejection or pain. While this shield may offer temporary relief, it ultimately blocks the genuine connection and fulfilment we all crave.

At the heart of healing lies authenticity. It is the key to building a life of purpose and connection. Recovery offers a unique opportunity to shed the masks we've worn and rediscover who we truly are. This process, though challenging, demands courage to face fears, doubts, and uncertainties. It is through embracing authenticity that we find the strength to loosen addiction's grip and reclaim our lives.

Honesty is the foundation of transformation. Acknowledging past mistakes, accepting our vulnerabilities, and aligning our lives with our values fosters trust and deepens our relationships. Engaging in activities that reflect our true selves – whether creative expression, nurturing relationships, or pursuing meaningful passions – reignites our inner light and strengthens our sense of self-worth.

Authenticity is not a destination – it is a lifelong journey. It requires self-compassion, patience, and a commitment to growth. The path may not be linear, but each step forward is a victory. Embrace the challenges, celebrate the moments of clarity, and remind yourself daily that you are deserving of love, connection, and joy.

As ancient Wayfinders charted courses across uncharted seas, you, too, are navigating your own unique path. Let their spirit of resilience, courage, and exploration inspire you as you embark on this transformative journey of recovery and self-discovery.

With warmest regards and unwavering support,

Vincenzia

CHAPTER TAKEAWAY

Unveiling the Complexity of Addiction

Addiction is far more than a matter of willpower or moral failing. It is a complex interplay of biological, psychological, and social factors, manifesting in forms that extend beyond substance abuse to include behavioural addictions.

This chapter has revealed how trauma, stress, and emotional dysregulation contribute to the development of addiction. By addressing underlying issues such as attachment styles and adverse childhood experiences (ACEs), we can foster a deeper understanding of addiction and create a foundation for effective recovery.

Attachment vs. Authenticity: A Delicate Balance

Attachment and authenticity are two fundamental human needs that often intersect in complex ways.

- **Attachment**: Provides security, connection, and belonging through bonds with others
- **Authenticity**: Reflects individuality and self-expression, allowing us to live in alignment with our true selves

The Challenge of Balance

Balancing attachment and authenticity can be difficult. When attachment is prioritised over authenticity, we may suppress our true selves to maintain connection, leading to people-pleasing, co-dependency, and a loss of identity. Conversely, prioritising authenticity over attachment can lead to isolation and a lack of meaningful relationships.

The Power of Authentic Attachment

Authentic attachment combines deep, meaningful connections with self-expression and individuality. It requires vulnerability, honesty, and a willingness to embrace both oneself and others.

Steps to Cultivate Authentic Attachment

Practice Self-Awareness: Understand your needs, values, and boundaries.

Develop Self-Compassion: Treat yourself with kindness and understanding.

Communicate Honestly: Share your feelings and thoughts openly with others.

Set Healthy Boundaries: Protect your emotional and physical well-being.

Cultivate Mindfulness: Stay present and connect with your experiences.

CHAPTER 1 SUMMARY

Factors Influencing Addiction

Addiction stems from an intricate web of influences:

- **Biological**: Altered brain chemistry, changes in the reward system, and neuroplasticity.
- **Psychological**: Trauma, stress, and maladaptive coping mechanisms.
- **Social**: Peer pressure, family dynamics, and environmental factors like poverty and unemployment.

Root Causes of Addiction

Adverse Childhood Experiences (ACEs): Early trauma such as abuse, neglect, or household dysfunction increases vulnerability to addiction.

Attachment Styles: Insecure attachments in childhood influence susceptibility to addiction.

Cultivating Authenticity: A Guide to a More Fulfilling Life

Key Practices for Authentic Living

1. **Self-Awareness**: Tune into your feelings, needs, and values.
2. **Honest Self-Expression**: Embrace your truth and set healthy boundaries.
3. **Nurturing Relationships**: Surround yourself with supportive, accepting people.
4. **Self-Compassion**: Forgive yourself and celebrate your unique qualities.
5. **Seeking Support**: Therapy or support groups can aid in personal growth.
6. **Confronting Trauma**: Address unresolved childhood experiences to promote healing.

Tools and Exercises for Recovery

Self-Reflection and Journaling

- **Explore Your Past**: Identify significant events and traumas.
- **Examine Your Present**: Reflect on coping mechanisms and their impact.
- **Envision Your Future**: Set goals aligned with your authentic self.

Mindfulness and Meditation

- **Guided Meditation**: Use tools like apps to cultivate mindfulness and reduce stress.
- **Body Scan Meditation**: Focus on physical sensations to ground yourself in the present.
- **Compassion Meditation**: Direct loving-kindness towards yourself and others.

Resources for Your Journey

Books to Inspire and Educate

- *In the Realm of Hungry Ghosts* by Gabor Maté: Explores addiction, trauma, and societal factors.
- *Daring Greatly* by Brené Brown: Highlights the power of vulnerability and authenticity.
- *The Gifts of Imperfection* by Brené Brown: Offers tools for embracing imperfection and living wholeheartedly.

CHAPTER 2 - TRAUMA AS A CATALYST FOR ADDICTION

THE GOLDEN BUDDHA: A TALE OF HIDDEN TREASURE

Centuries ago, in the heart of Thailand, a magnificent golden Buddha statue lay hidden beneath layers of plaster. This remarkable piece of history, concealed for generations, serves as a powerful metaphor for the hidden depths of the human psyche, particularly in the context of addiction and trauma.

During a tumultuous period in Thai history, monks feared for the safety of this precious artefact. To protect it from potential harm, they devised an ingenious plan: they covered the statue in layers of plaster, disguising it as an ordinary, unassuming clay Buddha. For centuries, this remarkable statue remained hidden from the world, its true nature concealed beneath a mundane exterior.

In 1957, as the monastery prepared to relocate, the monks began the arduous task of moving the seemingly ordinary clay Buddha. As they carefully lifted the statue, a crack appeared, revealing a glimpse of the golden treasure beneath. Intrigued, the monks continued to chip away at the plaster, uncovering layer by layer the breathtaking golden figure.

The discovery of the Golden Buddha captivated the nation and the world. It became a symbol of resilience, perseverance, and the enduring power of faith. This awe-inspiring tale serves as a reminder that true value often lies hidden beneath the surface, waiting to be discovered.

The story of the Golden Buddha is a powerful metaphor for the human spirit. Just as the Buddha's golden essence was hidden beneath layers of plaster, our true selves can become obscured by addiction and trauma.

Addiction and trauma can create a false self, a persona designed to protect us from pain and vulnerability. However, beneath this façade lies our authentic self, a radiant and resilient core. By delving into the depths of our experiences, we can begin to chip away the layers of conditioning and uncover our true nature.

In this chapter, we'll explore how childhood trauma can shape our adult behaviours and contribute to addiction. By understanding the root causes of our struggles, we can begin to heal and transform our lives.

THE DEFINITION OF TRAUMA

Trauma is not merely an event that occurred in the past – it is the enduring imprint that this event leaves on the mind, body, and spirit. This definition, popularised by renowned trauma expert Bessel van der Kolk, highlights the lasting impact of traumatic experiences. Trauma can be a deeply distressing event that overwhelms a person's ability to cope, threatening their sense of safety and security.

The psychological and physiological effects of trauma can be devastating. It can lead to a range of symptoms, including anxiety, depression, post-traumatic stress disorder (PTSD), and substance abuse. Trauma can also manifest physically, causing chronic pain, digestive issues, and other health problems.

It is important to recognise that trauma is a subjective experience. What one person considers traumatic may not be perceived as such by another. Additionally, the impact of trauma can vary widely from person to person. Some people may recover relatively quickly, while others may struggle with the effects for years.

In the following chapters, we will delve deeper into the personal experiences of people who have been affected by trauma. By sharing their stories, we hope to shed light on the complex nature of trauma and the power of healing.

A CASE STUDY OF EARLY CHILDHOOD TRAUMA

The Impact of Early Separation

Following the birth of her third child, Gabriel, Jean's health necessitated an extended hospital stay. With a demanding career and the responsibility of caring for their two older sons, Jean's husband, Grant, reluctantly entrusted Gabriel's care to his elderly grandmother. Despite her best intentions, the grandmother's rigid parenting style and lack of emotional attunement created a challenging environment for the infant. Gabriel was often left to soothe himself, a practice that can lead to feelings of isolation and insecurity.

Jean's frequent hospitalisations further disrupted Gabriel's sense of security and stability. The constant transitions between caregivers created confusion and anxiety, leaving him feeling abandoned and alone. As a result, Gabriel developed maladaptive coping mechanisms, such as emotional withdrawal and avoidance, to protect himself from further hurt.

Years later, Gabriel's parents were shocked to learn that their son was struggling academically and socially. Therapy revealed the underlying emotional wounds caused by his early childhood experiences. Despite their best intentions, their actions, or rather, inactions, had inadvertently contributed to his emotional distress.

This case study highlights the overpowering impact of early childhood experiences on an individual's development. Even seemingly minor disruptions in a child's early years can have long-lasting consequences. By understanding the complex interplay between attachment, trauma, and emotional regulation, we can better support children and help them heal from the wounds of the past.

Trauma's Footprint: Understanding Attachments, Behaviours, and Identities

As Gabor Maté poignantly states, "Trauma is not what happens to you; it is what happens inside you as a result of what happened to you." Traumatic experiences can sever our connection to ourselves and the world around us, leaving us feeling isolated and disconnected. This disconnection can manifest in various ways, including maladaptive coping mechanisms and distorted perceptions of reality.

The Role of Implicit Memory

Implicit memory, a powerful force that operates outside conscious awareness, plays a significant role in shaping our behaviours and beliefs. In the case of Gabriel, his early experiences of separation and neglect were deeply imprinted on his subconscious mind, influencing his later relationships and emotional responses.

Maladaptive Coping Mechanisms and Addiction

When we struggle to cope with the emotional pain of trauma, we may turn to maladaptive coping mechanisms, such as substance abuse, compulsive behaviours, or self-destructive habits. These behaviours provide temporary relief but ultimately exacerbate underlying issues.

The Path to Healing

To overcome the effects of trauma, it is essential to seek professional help and engage in therapeutic interventions. Through therapy, coaching, or counselling, we can gain insight into our past experiences, develop healthy coping mechanisms, and cultivate a stronger sense of self. By addressing the root causes of trauma, we can break free from the cycle of addiction and create a more fulfilling life.

Healing is a journey, not a destination. With patience, perseverance, and the support of others, it is possible to overcome the challenges of trauma and emerge stronger and more resilient.

The Hidden Self

Lindiwe had always been a people-pleaser, a habit ingrained in her from a young age. Growing up in a chaotic, alcohol-fuelled household, she learned to suppress her own needs and over function to maintain stability and peace and avoid conflict. She often felt overburdened yet invisible, her voice unheard, and her emotions dismissed. Consequently, she became perfectionistic and developed a deep-seated fear of rejection.

As an adult, Lindiwe found herself in a cycle of unhealthy relationships and self-destructive behaviours. She would regularly end up in relationships with demanding yet emotionally unavailable partners, desperately seeking love and acceptance. She would go to great lengths to please them, sacrificing her own needs and desires.

One day, a chance encounter with a Life Coach led Lindiwe on a journey of self-discovery. Through inquiry, she began to uncover the deep-rooted trauma of her childhood and the ways in which it had shaped her adult life. She learned to recognise the patterns of behaviour that had been holding her back and to challenge the negative beliefs she held about herself.

With each coaching session, Lindiwe chipped away at the layers of her false self, revealing the authentic person beneath. She learned to set boundaries, communicate her needs assertively, and prioritise her own well-being. As she embraced her true self, she began to attract healthier relationships and experiences.

Lindiwe's story is proof of the power of healing. By understanding the impact of early childhood trauma, we can break free from the chains of the past and embrace a more authentic and fulfilling future.

The Unconscious Mind and Trauma

Our brains are wired to prioritise survival and seek safety. In early childhood, experiences play a crucial role in shaping neural pathways that influence how we perceive and respond to the world. Traumatic experiences, such as neglect, abuse, or emotional deprivation, can disrupt this natural process, leading to maladaptive coping mechanisms that persist into adulthood.

Implicit memory, which operates outside of conscious awareness, has a powerful impact on shaping our behaviours and beliefs. Early childhood traumas often become deeply embedded in implicit memory, influencing thoughts, feelings, and actions without conscious recognition. These imprints, while protective at the time, can create patterns of avoidance, fear, and self-doubt that hinder emotional well-being later in life.

The Impact of Trauma on Behaviour and Identity

Trauma manifests in various ways that can profoundly shape behaviour and self-perception:

- **Relationship Patterns**: Difficulty forming and maintaining healthy connections, fear of intimacy, and a tendency toward co-dependency or controlling behaviours.
- **Addictive Behaviours**: Turning to substance abuse, compulsive habits, or other addictions to cope with unresolved emotional pain.
- **Emotional Dysregulation**: Challenges in managing emotions, often leading to outbursts, withdrawal, or emotional numbing.
- **Negative Self-Perception**: Persistent low self-esteem, self-doubt, and feelings of worthlessness.

HEALING FROM TRAUMA

Healing from trauma involves uncovering the layers of pain and addressing their root causes. With the right tools and support, we can transform our lives by:

- **Uncovering and Processing Trauma**: Exploring past experiences to develop healthier coping mechanisms.
- **Challenging Negative Beliefs**: Replacing self-limiting thoughts with positive affirmations and self-compassion.
- **Building Resilience:** Learning skills to manage stress, adversity, and change.
- **Nurturing Healthy Relationships**: Developing authentic connections built on trust and mutual understanding.

By confronting the past and embracing the present, we can emerge from the shadows of trauma and create a more fulfilling and empowered life.

FRACTURED SOCIETIES AND HISTORICAL TRAUMA

Addiction is not only a personal struggle but also a reflection of societal wounds. Historical traumas within families and communities contribute to cycles of marginalisation, poverty, and despair, creating fertile ground for addiction. The interconnectedness between individual and community well-being is undeniable:

healing oneself strengthens the community, and a healthier community promotes personal recovery.

United States: The Legacy of Slavery and Systemic Racism

The legacy of slavery and systemic racism has inflicted profound trauma on Black communities in the United States. The enduring effects of slavery, Jim Crow laws, and ongoing discrimination have resulted in high rates of addiction, mental health challenges, and incarceration.

Australia: Indigenous Peoples and Stolen Generations

The forced removal of Indigenous children from their families, known as the Stolen Generations, has left lasting scars. This historical injustice has contributed to intergenerational trauma, addiction, and mental health issues within Indigenous communities.

Ireland: The Famine and Its Aftermath

The Great Famine of the 1840s devastated Irish society, resulting in widespread starvation, disease, and emigration. The trauma of this period continues to influence Irish culture and identity, contributing to ongoing social and emotional challenges.

Understanding these historical and cultural contexts allows for the development of more effective strategies to prevent and treat addiction. Addressing root causes such as trauma, poverty, and inequality is essential for creating a healthier and more equitable society.

EPIGENETICS: A BRIDGE BETWEEN GENERATIONS

Epigenetics provides a fascinating lens to understand how trauma impacts not only individuals but also future generations. This field explores how environmental factors influence gene expression without altering the underlying DNA sequence – much like a dimmer switch that turns genes on or off.

How Does It Work?

Epigenetic modifications can be shaped by factors such as diet, stress, and exposure to toxins. These changes alter how genes are expressed, affecting physical traits, behaviours, and susceptibility to diseases.

The Impact of Trauma

Trauma is one of the most powerful influences on epigenetics. When we experience a traumatic event, the body releases stress hormones that can alter gene expression. These changes are often passed down to subsequent generations, impacting their physical and mental health.

For example, studies on Holocaust survivors have shown that their children exhibit altered stress responses. This suggests that the trauma endured by their parents has had a measurable impact on their genetic expression.

Understanding epigenetics emphasises the importance of addressing trauma holistically, not only to heal individuals but also to break the cycle of inherited vulnerabilities. This knowledge reinforces the power of healing – for ourselves and for future generations.

UNDERSTANDING PERSONALITY PATTERNS THROUGH THE LENS OF ATTACHMENT THEORY

Gordon Neufeld, a renowned clinical psychologist, offers an insightful framework for understanding how early childhood experiences shape adult behaviours.

Through the lens of attachment theory, we gain more understanding of the underlying motivations behind actions and relationships.

Attachment Styles and Personality Patterns

- **Anxious-Preoccupied**: People with this attachment style seek constant reassurance and validation. They are often overly sensitive to rejection and have difficulty trusting others.
- **Avoidant-Dismissive**: These individuals tend to avoid intimacy and emotional closeness, regularly appearing distant and aloof. Independence takes precedence over connection.
- **Fearful-Avoidant**: Characterised by a desire for intimacy combined with a fear of rejection, people with this attachment style may struggle to balance closeness and autonomy.

Unpacking Maladaptive Behaviours

Early experiences can lead to coping mechanisms that, while protective in childhood, become maladaptive in adulthood. Common examples include:

People-Pleasing: A relentless need for approval and conflict avoidance.

Perfectionism: An excessive drive to achieve and an intense fear of failure.

Control-Seeking: The need to exert control over situations and people to feel secure.

Self-Sabotage: Engaging in self-defeating behaviours that hinder success.

The Importance of Self-Awareness

Recognising that motivations may not always be as pure as they seem is a critical step toward self-awareness. While helping others can be fulfilling, actions driven by a need for external validation may ultimately leave us feeling empty. By practising mindfulness and reflection, we can identify our true motivations and align our actions with our core values and goals.

Reflective Prompts for Understanding Personality Patterns

To explore your personality patterns and their origins, reflect on the following questions:

Identifying Your Primary Attachment Style

- How do you typically respond to stress or conflict in relationships?
- Do you avoid intimacy or seek it excessively?
- How do you perceive yourself and your relationships?

Exploring Maladaptive Behaviours

- What are your most common coping mechanisms?
- Are there patterns of behaviour that lead to negative outcomes?
- How do you seek validation from others?

Understanding Your Motivations

- What are your core values and beliefs?
- How do your actions align with these values?
- Are your motivations intrinsic (internal) or extrinsic (external)?

Embracing Authenticity

- How can you nurture self-worth and self-acceptance?
- What steps can you take to develop healthier relationships?
- How can you challenge self-limiting beliefs and embrace vulnerability?

STORIES OF ADDICTION AND TRAUMA

Liam's Landscape: Navigating the Geography of Trauma and Addiction

I first met Liam when he was 10 years old. He was a bright-eyed boy, full of curiosity and energy, thriving on adventure and knowledge. However, beneath his vibrant exterior, his home life was turbulent. Constant arguments erupted into explosive anger, and his father eventually moved out, taking Liam's younger sister with him. Left alone to cope with his mother's erratic moods, Liam's resilience began to erode.

As time passed, Liam grew withdrawn. By his final year of school, he had developed a dependence on marijuana, using it to numb emotional pain and escape harsh realities. His substance use affected his academics, relationships, and overall well-being.

Liam's story illustrates how unresolved trauma can lead to addiction. As Gabor Maté emphasises, addressing addiction requires delving into the underlying pain that drives it. By understanding the root causes, we can develop effective strategies to heal trauma, nurture resilience, and build healthier coping mechanisms.

James' Journey of Seeking Refuge

When James first came to me, he shared his harrowing battle with crystal meth addiction, confessing to using the drug up to 15 times a day. For James, the drug was more than a substance – it was a source of transformation. It made him feel confident, alive, and invincible, temporarily washing away his emotional pain.

James's upbringing was fraught with challenges. He grew up under the oppressive rule of an abusive stepfather who withheld approval and inflicted relentless criticism. These experiences left James feeling profoundly worthless, undeserving of love, and fundamentally broken. Crystal meth became his refuge, offering a fleeting escape from self-doubt and a way to bridge the emotional chasm within.

James's journey highlights how addiction often emerges as a desperate response to emotional wounds. By addressing the trauma underlying addiction, we can move beyond judgement and help people heal.

Addiction as a Refuge

Addiction frequently provides a temporary refuge from life's challenges, creating an illusion of comfort and control. It offers relief from:

- **Emotional Pain**: Numbing anxiety, depression, or grief.
- **Physical Discomfort**: Easing chronic or acute physical pain.
- **Boredom or Loneliness**: Distracting from isolation or providing a fleeting sense of connection.
- **Low Self-Esteem**: Temporarily masking feelings of inadequacy.

Understanding these motivations is essential for effective treatment. By addressing the underlying causes, such as trauma, stress, and mental health challenges, we can empower people to break free from addiction and build healthier, more fulfilling lives.

THE BIOPSYCHOSOCIAL MODEL

A Story About Interconnectedness: The Biopsychosocial Analogy

Introducing a plant into your living space sparks an incredible change. It transitions from being just a decorative piece to a vibrant, living organism that flourishes under your attentive care.

As time passes, your beloved plant may start to wither and die. As a devoted caretaker, you may find yourself taking on the role of a detective, working to discover the underlying reasons for its deterioration. You might begin by investigating the basics: water, sunlight, and soil. Are you watering it appropriately? Is it receiving the right amount of sunlight? Is the soil rich enough to support its growth? Each question guides your actions, whether adjusting watering schedules, repositioning the plant for better light, or repotting it in nutrient-rich soil.

This process of nurturing a struggling plant mirrors the principles of the biopsychosocial model in human health. Just as the health of a plant depends on multiple interconnected factors, so does human well-being. By observing, learning, and adjusting our approaches, we recognise the intricate interplay between biological, psychological, and social influences in shaping health outcomes.

This analogy serves as a reminder to extend the same compassion and understanding to ourselves and others. Humans are far more complex than plants, with multifaceted emotional, psychological, and social needs. Moving beyond quick fixes and simplistic solutions, we must embrace a holistic approach to healing that accounts for the full spectrum of human experiences.

The Biopsychosocial Model

The biopsychosocial model highlights the interconnectedness of biological, psychological, and social factors in shaping mental health. It provides a holistic framework for understanding and addressing the complexities of human well-being.

Mental Health Beyond the Diagnosis: A Holistic Approach

In healthcare, there's often a tendency to rush to diagnose without fully exploring the underlying causes of symptoms. This can lead to misdiagnoses, particularly for individuals grappling with trauma and addiction. For example, unresolved trauma might be mistaken for bipolar disorder, while kinaesthetic learners could be incorrectly labelled with ADHD.

Sir Ken Robinson highlights the importance of rejecting one-size-fits-all approaches in education and mental health, advocating instead for personalised, holistic care. The biopsychosocial model enables a deeper understanding of the root causes of mental health challenges, addressing biological, psychological, and social dimensions alongside the impact of trauma and experiences.

Challenging the Framework: Critiques of the DSM-5 in Mental Health

The DSM-5, a key resource in psychiatry, has faced criticism for its limitations. Critics argue that its categorical approach oversimplifies mental health conditions, often neglecting the nuanced experiences of people. By focusing on symptoms rather than underlying causes, the DSM-5 risks medicalising normal human experiences and under-representing the effects of developmental trauma.

A biopsychosocial perspective offers a compelling alternative. It values the fluidity and uniqueness of individual experiences, fostering more compassionate and effective treatment plans that go beyond rigid diagnostic labels.

A Call to Reframe the Narrative: Shaping a Compassionate Path to Healing

Identifying solely as an "addict" can inadvertently reinforce self-defeating identities, limiting potential and obstructing recovery. Addiction is a temporary challenge, not a defining characteristic. Self-limiting narratives and negative beliefs can perpetuate addiction: thinking "I am an addict" merges your identity with the addiction; believing "I can't control my addiction" fosters a sense of powerlessness; thinking "I'll never overcome this" nurtures a fatalistic outlook; believing "I'm a failure because I'm an addict" heightens feelings of shame and stigma; and thinking "This is just who I am" hinders personal growth.

The Problem with Labels

Labelling people as "addicts" oversimplifies their struggles, ignoring the interplay of biological, psychological, and social factors. By focusing on the person rather than the label, we unlock opportunities for understanding, growth, and healing.

Labels Related to Identity

- **Victim**: Implies helplessness and can inhibit empowerment.
- **Broken**: Suggests irreparability and diminishes self-worth.
- **Failure**: Neglects achievements and potential for improvement.
- **Unworthy**: Reinforces feelings of low self-esteem and discourages self-care.
- **Weak**: Overlooks resilience and capacity for growth.

Labels Related to Behaviour

- **Lazy**: Ignores underlying challenges like burnout or mental health struggles.
- **Overthinker**: Minimises the complexity of analytical or cautious thinking.
- **Impulsive**: Misses the context behind spontaneous behaviour or decisions.
- **Procrastinator**: Overlooks factors like fear of failure or overwhelm.

Labels Related to Mental Health

- **Depressed**: Reduces a dynamic emotional experience to a static state.
- **Anxious**: Fails to acknowledge moments of calm or coping skills.
- **Traumatised**: Emphasises past pain rather than healing and resilience.

Labels Related to Social Perception

- **Difficult**: Ignores communication struggles or personal needs.
- **Outcast**: Reinforces isolation rather than encouraging inclusion.
- **People-pleaser**: Neglects the motivations for seeking harmony in relationships.
- **Stubborn**: Minimises determination and the capacity for thoughtful change.

Labels Related to Skills and Abilities

- **Untalented**: Dismisses potential for learning and skill development.
- **Unintelligent**: Neglects diverse forms of intelligence and problem-solving.
- **Inept**: Overlooks the value of practice and perseverance.
- **Uncreative**: Misses the unique ways individuals express creativity.

Labels Related to Relationships

- **Co-dependent**: Simplifies complex relational dynamics.
- **Lonely**: Ignores moments of connection or progress in building relationships.
- **Isolated**: Reduces a temporary state to a defining characteristic.

Labels Related to Addiction

- **Addict**: Oversimplifies a multifaceted challenge, focusing solely on the struggle.
- **Relapser**: Dismisses recovery efforts and the nonlinear nature of healing.
- **Dependent**: Ignores the process of building autonomy and resilience.

Labels Related to Societal Expectations

- **Underachiever**: Ignores the context of circumstances or different paths to success.
- **Perfectionist**: Stigmatises high standards without exploring underlying motivations.
- **Misfit**: Fails to appreciate individuality and unique contributions.

By acknowledging the complexity of each person's experience, we open doors to empowerment, growth, and healing. Reframing identities with strengths-based language encourages self-compassion and the belief that change is always possible. For example:

- Instead of "addict", try "person on a recovery journey".
- Instead of "failure", consider "someone learning through challenges".
- Replace "broken" with "resilient and healing".

Reclaiming Your Power: Strategies for Reframing

- **Challenge Negative Thoughts**: Replace self-defeating beliefs with empowering truths.
- **Practice Self-Compassion**: Treat yourself with kindness and understanding.
- **Set Realistic Goals**: Break the recovery journey into manageable steps.
- **Celebrate Progress**: Recognise even small successes.
- **Build Support Networks**: Surround yourself with understanding, uplifting people.
- **Seek Professional Help**: Work with therapists or counsellors to develop tools for growth.
- **Embrace Mindfulness**: Practice staying present and reducing stress.

Language Shapes Perception

Adopting person-centred language emphasises growth and resilience. For instance, rather than labelling someone with "C-PTSD", consider terms like Journey of Healing from Complex Trauma. This shift encourages empowerment and reframes recovery as an opportunity for transformation.

Rewriting Your Story: Practical Steps

1. **Identify Unhelpful Stories**: Reflect on beliefs such as "I'm not good enough" or "I'll never recover".
2. **Challenge Limiting Beliefs**: Examine the evidence for and against these thoughts.
3. **Craft a New Narrative**: Focus on strengths, growth, and the person you want to become.
4. **Share Your Story**: Build connections through support groups, therapy, or trusted relationships.

Language Matters: Alternatives for Labels

- **Trauma-Focused Terminology**: Replace stigmatising terms with compassionate alternatives.
- **Empowering Phrases**: Highlight resilience, growth, and the journey toward healing.

By reframing the narratives surrounding mental health and addiction, we create space for healing, understanding, and a more compassionate path forward. This biopsychosocial perspective reminds us that recovery is not about fitting into predefined categories but embracing the complexity of the human experience.

MY PERSONAL JOURNEY WITH COMPLEX TRAUMA: IMPACT, RESILIENCE, AND HEALING

From a young age, I found myself wrestling with the challenges of dyslexia. The classroom became a battleground where my struggles were met with bullying, ridicule, and academic failure. These formative experiences etched deep scars on my psyche, encouraging shame, low self-esteem, and social isolation. Despite my determination to persevere, the constant uphill battle laid the groundwork for trauma to take root, creating a foundation for the tumultuous journey that followed.

Dyslexia did not merely affect my academic life – it permeated every aspect of my existence, influencing relationships with family, friends, and peers. Perceived underachievement strained familial bonds, fostering tension and rejection. The chronic stress of navigating a world unaccommodating to my needs amplified feelings of inadequacy and shame. These challenges shaped the emergence of a negative self-concept, making me vulnerable to trauma-related symptoms.

As I grew older, the psychological burden compounded. Secondary trauma emerged as a significant force in my life, born from experiences of violence and crime. These harrowing events added weight to my emotional load, yet amidst the darkness, I clung to resilience and hope. I embarked on a journey of self-discovery fraught with obstacles: misdiagnoses, inadequate support, and a lack of resources.

Despite these struggles, my experience stresses a crucial truth: complex trauma can arise even in the presence of stable homes and loving parents. It is not confined to extreme violence or war but can stem from childhood adversity, interpersonal trauma, and ongoing stressors. My story highlights the interplay between learning challenges, neurodiversity, and trauma, offering a perspective on how these forces shape mental health outcomes.

HEALING TRAUMA AND ADDICTION: A JOURNEY OF MIND, BODY, AND SPIRIT

Traditional mental health approaches often prioritise the mind, overlooking the interconnectedness of mental, physical, and emotional well-being. Psychosomatic therapies provide a holistic framework for healing, integrating the mind, body, and spirit to address the complexities of trauma and addiction.

A Holistic Approach to Well-Being

Psychosomatic therapies go beyond symptom management, promoting overall health by addressing the root causes of distress. Techniques like mindfulness meditation, relaxation exercises, and biofeedback empower us to actively participate in our healing journey, fostering resilience and self-efficacy.

Culturally Sensitive and Tailored Interventions

Recognising the significance of cultural and social contexts, these therapies emphasise culturally sensitive approaches that respect diverse beliefs and practices. Integrating cultural healing traditions and addressing social determinants of health ensures interventions are both effective and inclusive.

Examples of Powerful Techniques

- **Mindfulness-Based Stress Reduction (MBSR):** Combines meditation and yoga to alleviate stress and enhance well-being.
- **Biofeedback**: Provides real-time physiological feedback, empowering individuals to manage symptoms like anxiety and chronic pain.
- **Compassionate Inquiry**: A mindfulness-based approach developed by Dr Gabor Maté, focusing on uncovering emotional roots and fostering self-awareness.

Expanding the Toolkit

- **Somatic Experiencing**: Addresses physical manifestations of trauma through body-centred techniques.
- **Expressive Arts Therapy**: Engages creativity to process emotions and release tension.
- **Emotional Freedom Technique (EFT)**: Combines acupressure with cognitive techniques to alleviate distress.
- **Hypnotherapy**: Accesses the subconscious to address underlying psychological factors.

A Call for a More Humane Approach to Mental Health

Mental health care must move beyond reductive diagnostic categories, embracing the individuality of each person's story. A nuanced approach considers personal history, cultural context, and social influences, creating treatment plans that resonate with each individual's unique journey.

THE POWER OF TRAUMA-INFORMED CARE

Trauma-informed care recognises the pervasive impact of trauma and emphasises safety, trust, and empowerment. By understanding how trauma affects both mind and body, we can create interventions that foster healing rather than perpetuating harm.

The Role of Mind-Body Practices like mindfulness, yoga, and meditation complement traditional therapies, helping reduce stress, improve emotional regulation, and promote overall resilience.

RECLAIMING OUR HUMANITY

Imagine a world where mental health care isn't just about symptom management but about cultivating resilience, self-awareness, and meaningful connection, where we look beyond labels to see the person and where trauma is met with compassion, not stigma. The story isn't just about what happened to us but how we rise.

What if we stopped asking, "What's wrong with you?" and instead asked, "What happened to you?" What if we chose to honour the complexity of human experience, embracing the messiness of healing as a powerful act of reclamation?

We live in a society that often prioritises efficiency over empathy and quick fixes over enduring solutions. Yet true healing demands depth. It requires us to confront the uncomfortable truths of our collective and individual pasts, to challenge systems that perpetuate harm, and to reimagine a future where the fullness of our humanity is celebrated.

This is the call to action: to rewrite the narrative, to redefine care, and to rekindle hope. Together, we can build a world where everyone has the opportunity not just to survive but to thrive. Will we answer that call?

Dear Fellow Traveller,

We all wear masks, don't we? Layers of protection carefully constructed over time to shield us from harm, rejection, and disappointment. Like the Golden Buddha, hidden beneath its layers of plaster for centuries, our true selves often lie obscured, waiting to be rediscovered.

These layers once served us well, protecting us during times of vulnerability and allowing us to grow in safety. But now, the time has come to embark on a journey of self-discovery. Together, let's mindfully and compassionately chip away at these defences, honouring the journey and embracing the pace at which our truths reveal themselves. Beneath the surface lies a treasure trove of potential, creativity, and love – a golden essence unique to each of us.

In this process, let's resist the urge to pathologise or label ourselves and others. Instead, let's approach our experiences with curiosity and compassion. By exploring the root causes of our behaviours and emotions, we can develop healthier coping mechanisms and cultivate a deep sense of self-acceptance.

As we walk this path together, let us offer one another support, understanding, and a safe space to be vulnerable. Let's share our stories and celebrate the richness of our unique journeys. In doing so, we will create a community where authenticity is honoured, and healing becomes a collective act of courage.

Are you ready to uncover your golden self? Are you ready to embrace your authentic being? Let's embark on this transformative journey together, with curiosity in our hearts and compassion as our guide.

With warmth and encouragement,

Vincenzia

CHAPTER 2 SUMMARY

THE IMPACT OF TRAUMA

- Trauma leaves lasting imprints on the mind, body, and spirit.
- It manifests in symptoms like anxiety, depression, PTSD, and substance abuse and can cause physical health issues such as chronic pain.
- Trauma is a subjective experience with varying impacts on individuals.

TRAUMA'S FOOTPRINT: UNDERSTANDING ATTACHMENTS, BEHAVIOURS, AND IDENTITIES

- Traumatic experiences sever connections with oneself and the world, fostering isolation.
- Implicit memory embeds trauma deeply, influencing behaviour and beliefs unconsciously.
- Maladaptive coping mechanisms, such as substance abuse or self-destructive habits, often develop as responses to trauma.

THE PATH TO HEALING

- Healing requires professional help, therapeutic interventions, mindfulness, and self-compassion.
- Recovery is a journey marked by patience, perseverance, and support.

IMPACT OF EARLY CHILDHOOD TRAUMA

- Early trauma shapes neural pathways, influencing perceptions and responses.
- Trauma is often stored in implicit memory, impacting thoughts, feelings, and actions unconsciously.

FRACTURED SOCIETIES AND HISTORICAL TRAUMA

Addiction reveals scars of historical trauma within families and communities.

Examples include the legacy of slavery in the U.S., the Stolen Generations in Australia, and the Irish Great Famine.

Understanding these contexts is essential for effective prevention and treatment strategies.

EPIGENETICS: A BRIDGE BETWEEN GENERATIONS

- Explores how environmental factors influence gene expression without altering DNA.
- Trauma can alter gene expression, affecting physical traits and behaviours across generations.

UNDERSTANDING PERSONALITY PATTERNS THROUGH ATTACHMENT THEORY

- Attachment styles: Anxious-Preoccupied, Avoidant-Dismissive, and Fearful-Avoidant – each shapes behaviours and relationships.
- Maladaptive coping mechanisms include people-pleasing, perfectionism, control-seeking, and self-sabotage.
- Self-awareness and mindfulness help uncover motivations and foster healthier choices.

STORIES OF ADDICTION AND TRAUMA

- Liam's Landscape: Used marijuana to numb pain and escape a turbulent home life.
- James' Journey: Crystal meth became James's refuge from unrelenting emotional abuse and feelings of inadequacy.

Both stories reveal addiction as a desperate response to emotional wounds.

ADDICTION AS A REFUGE

- Addiction offers temporary relief from emotional pain, physical discomfort, loneliness, and low self-esteem.

- Addressing underlying causes like trauma and mental health issues encourages lasting recovery.

THE BIOPSYCHOSOCIAL MODEL

Emphasises the interconnectedness of biological, psychological, and social factors.

A holistic perspective that addresses the whole person rather than focusing solely on symptoms.

MOVING BEYOND LABELS AND RECLAIMING POWER

- Labels like “addict” reinforce self-defeating narratives and hinder recovery.
- Strategies for reframing include challenging negative thoughts, practising self-compassion, and embracing mindfulness.
- Rewriting personal narratives nurtures empowerment and growth.

HEALING TRAUMA AND ADDICTION: A JOURNEY OF MIND, BODY, AND SPIRIT

- Psychosomatic therapies integrate mental, emotional, and physical healing.
- Techniques include mindfulness-based stress reduction, biofeedback, compassionate inquiry, and somatic experiencing.
- Culturally sensitive and tailored interventions respect diverse backgrounds and maximise effectiveness.

A CALL FOR A MORE HUMANE APPROACH TO MENTAL HEALTH

- Move beyond rigid diagnoses to consider personal histories and cultural contexts.

- Adopt trauma-informed care to create safe, supportive environments.
- Embrace mind-body practices like mindfulness and yoga to complement traditional therapies.

FINAL PROVOCATION: THE INVITATION TO TRANSFORM

This chapter explores the reality that trauma and addiction are not mere afflictions but also opportunities for powerful transformation. By chipping away at the layers of pain, we can uncover the golden core of our authentic selves. The question remains: Will we embrace the challenge to heal, grow, and redefine our lives, or will we remain encased in the plaster of past wounds? The path to recovery is not easy, but it is worth it – for within every person lies the potential to shine brighter than ever before.

REFLECTIVE PROMPTS

UNDERSTANDING TRAUMA

1. What personal experiences have left lasting imprints on your mind, body, or spirit?
2. How do you think trauma has influenced your behaviours, beliefs, or relationships?
3. Reflect on a time when you felt disconnected from yourself or the world. What contributed to this disconnection?

RECOGNISING TRAUMA'S IMPACT

1. What maladaptive coping mechanisms have you observed in yourself or others as a response to pain or trauma?
2. How has trauma influenced your ability to form or maintain healthy attachments?
3. Consider how implicit memories may shape your unconscious behaviours or reactions. Can you identify specific examples?

THE PATH TO HEALING

1. What steps have you taken – or can you take – to address the emotional and physical effects of trauma?
2. How can mindfulness or self-compassion support you in your recovery journey?
3. Who or what in your life provides the patience and support necessary for healing?

EARLY CHILDHOOD AND GENERATIONAL TRAUMA

1. Reflect on your childhood. Were there unmet needs or experiences that might have influenced your current patterns?
2. How do you think generational trauma has affected your family's dynamics or your personal development?
3. What steps can you take to address and disrupt patterns of trauma in your life or family?

UNDERSTANDING ADDICTION AS A RESPONSE TO PAIN

1. How has addiction – or other maladaptive behaviour(s) – served as a refuge or coping mechanism for you or someone you know?
2. Reflect on the ways in which addiction might be masking underlying pain or unmet needs in your life.
3. What would it look like to address the root causes of addictive behaviours rather than the symptoms?

REFRAMING PERSONAL NARRATIVES

1. Are there labels or self-defeating narratives that you've internalised? How might you begin to rewrite your story?
2. What does empowerment look like for you? How can you reclaim power in areas where you've felt diminished?

HEALING AND GROWTH

1. Consider the biopsychosocial model. How might addressing biological, psychological, and social factors create a more holistic approach to your healing?
2. What role do you see for community, spirituality, or nature in your journey toward recovery and growth?
3. How might you transform past pain into an opportunity for growth and self-discovery?

TOOLS AND RESOURCES

TOOLS

- **TRAUMA-INFORMED CARE TRAINING**

Develop the skills to create healing environments by understanding how trauma impacts the mind and body. This is ideal for professionals and caregivers aiming to provide compassionate and effective support.

- **THERAPEUTIC MODALITIES**

Explore evidence-based approaches tailored to address trauma and addiction:

- CBT (Cognitive Behavioural Therapy): Helps identify and reframe negative thought patterns.
- EMDR (Eye Movement Desensitisation and Reprocessing): A proven method for processing and healing trauma.
- DBT (Dialectical Behaviour Therapy): Focuses on improving emotional regulation, distress tolerance, and relationship skills.
- MBSR (Mindfulness-Based Stress Reduction): Combines mindfulness and meditation to reduce stress and improve well-being.

- **SUPPORT GROUPS**

Connect with addiction- and trauma-focused groups to share experiences, receive emotional support, and build a sense of community.

- **MENTAL HEALTH SCREENINGS**

Use tools like the Adverse Childhood Experiences (ACEs) questionnaire to uncover trauma-related risks and gain insights into personal patterns.

- **MINDFULNESS APPS**

Leverage apps like Headspace and Calm for guided meditations and techniques to enhance emotional regulation and resilience.

- **COMMUNITY RESOURCES**

Reach out to local counselling centres, crisis hotlines, and outreach programs for tailored support and guidance.

- **BIOPSYCHOSOCIAL ASSESSMENTS**

Employ comprehensive tools to evaluate physical, mental, and social needs, fostering a holistic understanding of individual well-being.

BOOKS

- ***The Body Keeps the Score*** by Bessel van der Kolk
  Explores trauma's impact on mind and body, offering therapeutic insights.

- ***Complex PTSD: From Surviving to Thriving*** by Pete Walker
  A practical guide to recovering from childhood trauma.

- ***Waking the Tiger*** by Peter Levine
  Focuses on healing trauma by addressing bodily responses.

- ***What My Bones Know*** by Stephanie Foo
  A memoir that delves into healing from complex trauma.

- ***The Myth of Normal*** by Dr Gabor Maté
  Examines how trauma impacts mental and physical health.

- ***When the Body Says No*** by Dr Gabor Maté
  Highlights the connection between stress, emotions, and physical illness.

- ***Addiction as an Attachment Disorder*** by Philip J. Flores
  Explores the relationship between attachment issues and addiction.

- ***Memoirs of an Addicted Brain*** by Marc Lewis
  A neuroscientist's personal journey through addiction and recovery.

YOUTUBE RESOURCES

- **The Science of Addiction** (AsapSCIENCE)
  Simplifies addiction's neurological underpinnings for accessible understanding.

- **Addiction** (Kurzgesagt)
  Explores the causes and science behind addiction in a visually engaging way.

- TEDx Talks on Addiction
  Features expert insights and inspiring personal recovery stories.

- **The Biology of Trauma** (Dr Nadine Burke Harris)
  Explains trauma's long-term effects on physical and mental health.
- **Healing from Trauma** (Dr Judith Herman)
- Discusses the courage and steps necessary for trauma recovery.
- **Complex PTSD: From Surviving to Thriving** (Pete Walker)
- Provides insights on healing Complex PTSD through practical strategies.
- Biopsychosocial Model of Health and Illness
- Explores holistic healthcare approaches that integrate biological, psychological, and social dimensions.

CHAPTER 3 - THE PLEASURE PRINCIPLE AND THE PAIN AVOIDANCE MECHANISM

THE PURSUIT OF PLEASURE AND THE AVOIDANCE OF PAIN

The human experience is deeply influenced by two fundamental motivations: the pursuit of pleasure and the avoidance of pain. These primal drives, rooted in our evolutionary history, shape our behaviours, emotions, and decision-making processes. Central to these motivations is a complex neurochemical system, with dopamine playing a pivotal role.

Dopamine, often referred to as the "reward neurotransmitter", is released in the brain's reward pathway when we experience pleasure or anticipate a reward. This neurochemical response reinforces behaviours that lead to positive outcomes, such as eating, socialising, and achieving goals. However, when dopamine levels become dysregulated, it can drive addictive behaviours and compulsive seeking of pleasure.

This chapter explores the intricate relationship between dopamine, pleasure, and pain. By understanding how this neurotransmitter influences our motivations and behaviours, we can gain an in-depth understanding of addiction, mental health challenges, and the pursuit of happiness.

The Monkey and the Banana: A Tale of Dopamine and Addiction

A hollowed-out coconut with a ripe banana inside lures a curious monkey. The monkey reaches in and grasps the banana but cannot withdraw her hand due to the narrow opening. Despite the discomfort and obvious potential for escape, the monkey remains trapped, unable to let go.

This simple story mirrors the complex nature of addiction. The initial pleasure or relief that a substance or behaviour provides can be overwhelmingly powerful, leading to compulsive seeking. Over time, as the addiction deepens, we become trapped in a cycle of harmful behaviour, unable to break free despite negative consequences.

THE DOPAMINE TRAP

At the core of this struggle lies dopamine, a neurotransmitter responsible for reward and motivation. When we engage in pleasurable activities, dopamine is released, creating a sense of euphoria and reinforcing the behaviour. Addictive substances and behaviours, however, hijack this natural reward system, flooding the brain with dopamine and creating an artificial sense of reward.

Over time, the brain adapts by reducing its sensitivity to dopamine, making natural rewards less pleasurable. This drives us to seek ever-increasing amounts of the addictive substance or behaviour, perpetuating the cycle of addiction.

BREAKING FREE FROM THE CYCLE

Recovery is possible by understanding the neurobiological mechanisms behind addiction and seeking appropriate support. Therapy, medication, and support groups can provide the tools necessary to break free from addiction.

Like the monkey who must release the banana to regain freedom, we must learn to let go of harmful behaviours and embrace healthier alternatives. Mindfulness, self-compassion, and a supportive network are essential tools for overcoming addiction and building a fulfilling life.

DOPAMINE: SEEKING PLEASURE AND AVOIDING PAIN

The human brain's intricate network of neurons and signalling molecules is shaped by neuromodulators like dopamine, which play a key role in motivation, learning, and behaviour. Dopamine regulates the brain's reward and pleasure pathways, reinforcing actions that lead to satisfaction and survival.

However, addictive substances and behaviours disrupt this system. They trigger abnormal surges of dopamine, overshadowing natural rewards. As a result, we become trapped in a cycle of dependency, requiring increasing amounts of the substance or behaviour to feel normal, while natural rewards lose their appeal.

THE CYCLE OF ADDICTION

This dependency creates a vicious cycle.

1. We become reliant on the addictive substance or behaviour to feel normal.
2. Natural rewards lose their significance.

3. Despite negative consequences, the behaviour continues to avoid withdrawal or discomfort.

Breaking this cycle requires creating healthier pathways for seeking pleasure and coping with pain, laying the foundation for recovery and a healthier, more balanced life.

BEYOND THE FIX: FINDING LASTING FREEDOM FROM ADDICTION

"It is hard to get enough of something that almost works."

– Gabor Maté

Like many addictive behaviours, smoking offered me a deceptive promise. It almost relieved my tension and stress. It seemed to soothe my anxieties and felt like it worked – until it didn't. The temporary relief was never enough and could never be enough. Gabor Maté's revelatory insight captures the essence of addiction: a desperate grasp for a solution that ultimately falls short.

Addiction is more than substances or behaviours – it is a pursuit of a feeling – an escape, a numbing of pain, or a fleeting sense of fulfilment. The addictive cycle revolves around this "almost", where the promise of relief is just close enough to keep us hooked, yet always out of reach.

THE "ALMOST" BUT INSUFFICIENT SURGE OF DOPAMINE IN ADDICTION

Breaking free from addiction requires addressing its neurochemical roots. Recovery involves recalibrating the brain's dopamine balance, which has been hijacked by addictive behaviours or substances. This begins with abstinence and is reinforced by activities that promote natural dopamine release, such as mindfulness, physical exercise, meaningful social connections, and engaging hobbies.

As the brain resets its reward system, pleasure can gradually return to healthy, everyday activities. However, the allure of addiction lies in its "almost": the fleeting moments of relief that, for someone grappling with trauma, anxiety, or emptiness, can feel like a lifeline. This temporary solace, however, is inherently fleeting, often followed by deeper despair and a heightened compulsion to repeat the behaviour.

The "almost" solution traps us in a cycle of seeking that never satisfies us. It acts as a powerful reminder of an elusive goal, fuelling the need for more. This is why, as Dr Maté observes, it becomes nearly impossible to get enough. The object of addiction can never deliver lasting fulfilment, leaving us chasing an illusion of completion.

BEYOND THE "ALMOST": CONFRONTING THE ILLUSION

The false promise of relief also masks and exacerbates underlying issues. Instead of addressing the root causes of pain, addiction acts as a temporary bandage, preventing true healing. Over time, the addiction deepens, and the original problems – unresolved trauma, unmet needs, or emotional pain – fester beneath the surface.

Breaking this cycle requires recognising the "almost" for what it truly is: an illusion. It involves facing the underlying issues, seeking professional help, and adopting healthier coping mechanisms. This journey opens the door to genuine healing and a life no longer tethered to the insufficient "almost".

THE HUMAN DESIRE FOR PLEASURE AND AVERSION TO PAIN

Dr Anna Lembke, an addiction medicine specialist and author of Dopamine Nation, explains that humans are fundamentally driven by a desire to seek pleasure and avoid pain. This drive is deeply rooted in our evolutionary biology. For our ancestors, survival depended on finding food, forming social bonds, and securing shelter – activities that were both necessary and rewarding.

In modern times, however, this innate drive has been co-opted by substances and behaviours that exploit our reward systems. Smartphones, social media platforms, video games, fast food, online shopping, and streaming services provide instant gratification, triggering dopamine surges that mimic the rewards of natural survival behaviours. Substances like alcohol, nicotine, and drugs take this a step further, overwhelming the brain's reward system.

This creates a mismatch between our biology and our environment. While our ancestors thrived on balance and moderation, these modern stimuli hijack our brain's mechanisms, leading to compulsive overuse and dependency. Addiction thrives in this gap, where the natural pursuit of pleasure becomes distorted into harmful cycles of overconsumption and dependence.

Dr Lembke offers this wisdom:

"Humans are the ultimate seekers, but if we seek blindly, we will run into trouble."

Her words highlight the importance of mindful and intentional seeking. While curiosity and ambition are natural, blindly pursuing pleasure without considering risks or consequences can lead to harm. To live balanced and fulfilling lives, we must temper our seeking with wisdom and mindfulness, understanding the risks of naive or impulsive behaviours.

A BALANCED PURSUIT OF FULFILMENT

By understanding the interplay between dopamine and our seeking behaviour, we gain valuable insights into human nature and addiction. True freedom from addiction lies in moving beyond the temporary allure of the "almost" and embracing a more sustainable path toward fulfilment. This requires acknowledging the limits of external solutions and cultivating internal resilience, purpose, and joy.

EXPLORING HEALTHY DOPAMINE STIMULANTS: A GUIDE TO HEALTH-PROMOTING BEHAVIOURS

In today's world of instant gratification, finding healthy dopamine sources is key to well-being, especially in addiction recovery. A health-seeking mindset encourages behaviours that enhance or maintain health, prioritising long-term fulfilment over temporary rewards. This section explores how adopting a health-seeking attitude – focused on presence, delayed gratification, and mindful choices – supports a balanced lifestyle and sustainable dopamine regulation.

1. Being Present and Process-Focused

Health-seeking emphasises full engagement in the present moment, focusing on the process of well-being rather than only outcomes like weight loss or muscle gain. For instance, rather than exercising solely to reach a goal, you immerse yourself in the act of movement, appreciating how it strengthens your body and uplifts your mood.

This mindfulness-based approach reduces stress, improves emotional resilience, and nurtures a deeper connection with your health. Over time, this cultivates sustainable, positive habits that prioritise the joy and benefits of the journey rather than obsessing over the destination.

2. Delaying Immediate Gratification

In a society geared toward instant rewards, learning to prioritise long-term health over short-term pleasures is transformative. Choosing a walk in nature over scrolling through social media or opting for nutritious meals instead of sugary snacks may seem minor, but these choices recalibrate the brain's reward system.

Recognising the risks of immediate gratification not only helps break the cycle of overconsumption but also builds emotional resilience and self-discipline, essential tools for navigating life's challenges without falling into addictive patterns.

3. Optimising Dopamine Interaction

The goal of health-seeking is not to flood the brain with dopamine but to create sustainable, balanced interactions with this vital neurotransmitter. Practices like mindfulness, exercise, and meaningful connections stabilise dopamine levels, supporting a healthy reward system that isn't reliant on extreme stimulation.

By promoting this balance, you reduce the likelihood of addiction and develop a healthier relationship with pleasure and fulfilment. This approach allows you to meet your innate human desire for satisfaction while avoiding harmful overindulgence.

HEALTH-SEEKING BEHAVIOURS TO BOOST DOPAMINE

Physical Activities

- **Regular Exercise**: Engage in moderate-intensity activities such as walking, jogging, or cycling for at least 30 minutes most days. High-intensity interval training (HIIT) is particularly effective in enhancing dopamine release.
- **Dance or Movement**: Classes like Zumba, salsa, or even free-form dance tap into your body's rhythm, lifting mood and enhancing brain chemistry.
- **Nature Walks**: Combine physical activity with the calming effects of natural environments to amplify dopamine production and reduce stress.
- **Trying New Sports**: Activities like rock climbing, surfing, or martial arts challenge your body and mind, providing a dopamine boost through novelty and mastery.

Mental Exercises

- **Completing Tasks**: Checking items off a to-do list, no matter how small, triggers dopamine release and builds momentum for larger achievements.
- **Creative Pursuits**: Painting, writing, or playing a musical instrument engages your creativity and provides a sense of accomplishment.
- **Mindfulness or Meditation**: Regular meditation increases focus and self-awareness, promoting steady dopamine regulation over time.

- **Learning New Skills**: Tackling challenges like a new language or instrument activates the brain's reward system, fostering curiosity and growth.

Social Behaviour

- **Spending Time with Loved Ones**: Engaging in genuine, joyful interactions enhances dopamine and strengthens social bonds.
- **Acts of Kindness**: Helping others encourages a sense of purpose and triggers the brain's reward circuits.
- **Expressing Gratitude**: Focusing on what you're thankful for creates a positive outlook and uplifts your mood.
- **Celebrating Achievements**: Acknowledging and rewarding your successes reinforces positive behaviours.

Creative Pursuits

- **Creating Art**: Painting, sculpting, or drawing allows for self-expression while engaging dopamine pathways.
- **Music**: Learning to play an instrument or joining a choir can create profound joy as well as have cognitive benefits.
- **Workshops**: Joining community groups or classes introduces novelty and connection to creative activities.

Embrace the Cold

- **Cold Showers or Ice Baths**: Exposing yourself to cold water can trigger an adrenaline response, followed by a gradual increase in dopamine, improving mood and resilience.

TIPS FOR CHOOSING HEALTHY DOPAMINE SOURCES

- **Enjoyment**: Choose activities you genuinely love to maintain long-term motivation.
- **Challenge Yourself**: Seek opportunities to step outside your comfort zone – mastering challenges stimulates dopamine release and builds confidence.
- **Mix It Up**: Variety prevents boredom and keeps your brain engaged. Rotate between different activities to maintain interest and novelty.

CAUTION AGAINST OVER-SIMPLIFICATION

While these health-seeking behaviours are valuable, it's essential to recognise that lasting well-being is a holistic process. Balancing dopamine is about nurturing a stable, sustainable reward system. Therapy, addressing trauma, and building strong support systems are equally crucial components of overall health.

By integrating these practices with a mindful, compassionate attitude, you can create a life that is both fulfilling and resilient, aligning your desires for pleasure and growth with choices that support your long-term well-being.

HIJACKED HIGHWAYS: HOW NEURAL PATHWAYS FUEL ADDICTION

Addiction is closely linked to the development of neural pathways that regulate impulses and rewards. These pathways, part of the mesolimbic reward system, strongly influence our behaviour and decision-making.

The system consists of two key components:

1. **Impulse**: Located in the limbic system, including the amygdala and nucleus accumbens, this part triggers the "I want it now" feeling. When you encounter

something tempting, this area releases dopamine, the neurotransmitter tied to pleasure and motivation.

2. **Reward**: Found in the ventral striatum, this area releases dopamine when you achieve something rewarding, reinforcing the behaviour that led to the reward.

In essence, the impulse creates a craving, while the reward makes you feel good when you act on it.

THE PROBLEMATIC REINFORCEMENT LOOP

When engaging in addictive behaviours like substance use, the brain creates a reinforcement loop. The initial impulse triggers the behaviour and the reward reinforces it with dopamine, making it more likely you'll repeat the action.

Over time, these pathways become more entrenched with repeated behaviours. Imagine a well-worn path turning into a fast-moving highway in your brain. The neural connections become stronger, and the impulse to engage in addictive behaviours becomes harder to resist.

THE GRIP OF ADDICTION

Intensified Cravings: As these neural pathways strengthen, cravings become more intense. You may find it increasingly difficult to control the urge to engage in addictive behaviours, even when you understand the negative consequences.

Diminished Control: Addiction weakens your ability to exert self-control. The entrenched impulse and reward pathways overpower your rational decision-making, making it harder to quit or reduce addictive behaviours.

Negative Consequences: Addiction leads to severe consequences, including health problems, mental health challenges, financial difficulties, and strained relationships. The pursuit of the reward, driven by these pathways, perpetuates the cycle of addiction.

THE CRUCIAL ROLE OF DOPAMINE IN SURVIVAL: A THOUGHT-PROVOKING EXPERIMENT

In my research for my book, I came across a compelling experiment that highlights the critical role of dopamine in controlling essential survival behaviours such as seeking food and water. The experiment involved removing dopamine receptors from a mouse's brain. Without these receptors, the mouse stopped looking for food and water, ultimately leading to its death. This demonstrates the importance of dopamine in motivation, movement, and the reward and pleasure systems.

While the experiment provided valuable insights into dopamine's role in survival, it's important to acknowledge the ethical concerns surrounding animal testing. Many people, myself included, advocate for cruelty-free research methods.

Source:

Schultz, W. (1998). Predictive Reward Signal of Dopamine Neurons. Journal of Neurophysiology, 80(1), 1-27. This study elaborates on dopamine's role in motivation and reward systems and provides insights into how dopamine receptor dysfunction can affect survival behaviours in animals.

Wise, R. A. (2004). Dopamine, learning and motivation. Nature Reviews Neuroscience, 5(6), 483–494. https://doi.org/10.1038/nrn1406

Zhou, Q. Y., & Palmiter, R. D. (1995). Dopamine-deficient mice are severely hypoactive, adipsic, and aphagic. Cell, 83(7), 1197–1209. https://doi.org/10.1016/0092-8674(95)90145-0

Exploring the Experiment's Findings

The experiment's findings suggest that dopamine plays a vital role in driving animals, including humans, to perform essential tasks such as finding, obtaining, and consuming food and water. When dopamine receptors are damaged or removed, the brain's ability to communicate the significance of these essential activities is impaired, leading to a noticeable lack of motivation. In this case, the mouse's drive to seek food and water decreased due to dopamine receptor dysfunction. Consequently, the mouse ceased engaging in these life-sustaining behaviours, resulting in its death. This highlights dopamine's undeniable importance for survival. When dopamine function is compromised, motivation and drive diminish, jeopardising the ability to meet physiological needs. This deficit, as demonstrated in the experiment, can lead to serious health problems or even death.

THE BALANCING ACT: PLEASURE AND PAIN

Our brains are intricately designed, holding a fascinating truth: the same areas manage both pleasure and pain. This delicate balance is crucial for our survival and overall well-being. Deep within the complexity of our brains, a symphony of neural regions and pathways coordinates the processing of both pleasure and pain, achieving a remarkable cognitive feat by managing a wide range of emotions and sensory information.

Central to this neural performance is the dopaminergic system, which directs impulses toward pleasure and reward. Dopamine takes centre stage in the brain's elaborate reward circuits, orchestrating our deepest cravings and moments of pleasure. The concept of the "opponent process reaction" is akin to the rise and fall of emotional waves, playing out on the stage of our feelings. It follows a pattern where an initial stimulus triggers a series of emotions, often followed by an opposing emotional reaction. In the realm of pleasure and pain, experiences that reach ecstatic highs (pleasure) eventually descend to lower levels (pain), all in pursuit of emotional equilibrium.

Chasing the Dragon: A Homeostatic Perspective

The phrase "Chasing the Dragon" is a striking metaphor for the relentless pursuit of an initial euphoric high. Through the lens of homeostasis, we can understand this as a desperate attempt to restore a disrupted emotional equilibrium.

The Role of Homeostasis

Normally, our brains maintain a steady emotional state, much like a thermostat regulates temperature. This is our hedonic set point. However, when we introduce substances that hijack the brain's reward system, this delicate balance is upset.

The Addicted Brain

Addiction represents a homeostatic imbalance. The brain, in an attempt to counteract the overwhelming dopamine surge caused by the substance, down-regulates its dopamine receptors. This adaptation is the brain's way of restoring balance, but it comes at a cost:

- **Hedonic Set Point Shift**: The individual's baseline happiness is lowered. What once brought pleasure now feels neutral.
- **Tolerance**: To achieve the same euphoric effect, more of the substance is required, leading to increased consumption. This is the "chasing the dragon" part – the futile attempt to recapture the initial high.
- **Withdrawal**: When substance use stops, the brain, now accustomed to the altered state, reacts violently. Physical and emotional withdrawal symptoms occur as the brain tries to rebalance itself.

RECOVERY AS RESTORATION

Recovery is essentially the process of restoring homeostasis. The brain needs time to re-sensitise its dopamine receptors and rebuild its natural reward system.

This is a challenging process, often accompanied by cravings and emotional ups and downs.

In essence, "Chasing the Dragon" is a desperate attempt to artificially maintain an unsustainable level of pleasure, a battle against the brain's natural drive for equilibrium. Recovery is about re-establishing that balance and finding genuine sources of satisfaction and well-being.

THE CRAVING CONUNDRUM: HABITUATION AND STABILITY

The human mind is a complex labyrinth, and its intricate neural processes give rise to a range of fascinating phenomena, including cravings. These urges act as potent signals from our brains, pushing us to engage in behaviours that may not always align with our best interests. They represent a fundamental human drive to seek pleasure and restore balance. This relentless pursuit of an ideal emotional state, the hedonic set point, is a fundamental human drive that plays out throughout our lives. Despite the challenges posed by a world in perpetual change, our brains remain steadfast in their pursuit of balance and stability.

Habituation, the psychological phenomenon of diminishing responses to repeated stimuli, plays a crucial role in addiction. As you have come to learn, over time, the positive effects of addiction fade while the negative effects become more pronounced. Habituation is a powerful force in the downward spiral of addiction. It drives people to crave short-lived pleasures even more despite the mounting negative consequences. This is one of the reasons why addiction is so difficult to overcome.

THE COMPLEX DYNAMICS OF ADDICTION AND RESILIENCE

Anna Lembke challenges the moral view of addiction in Dopamine Nation, presenting it as a brain condition influenced by various factors that hijack the brain's reward system. This compulsive pursuit of pleasure is exacerbated by habituation, where repeated exposure to a stimulus diminishes its effectiveness. Lembke advocates for a process-oriented approach to life – prioritising the enjoyment of the journey over the mere achievement of goals. By appreciating the small joys and experiences that arise in our daily lives, we can prevent ourselves from becoming overly reliant on negative or unhelpful sources of pleasure. By understanding the neurobiology of addiction and adopting a process-oriented mindset, we can manage the intricate system of habits, finding lasting happiness not only in achieving goals but in the unfolding of the journey itself.

UNDERSTANDING CROSS-ADDICTION AND ANHEDONIA

Anhedonia is the inability to enjoy pleasurable or rewarding activities, such as hobbies, socialising, eating, or personal relationships. This condition results in a diminished quality of life and functional impairments. In addiction and recovery, anhedonia is prevalent. During active addiction, substances or behaviours (e.g., gambling or overeating) increase pleasure, overstimulating the brain's reward system. This overstimulation leads to anhedonia – a state where the brain becomes desensitised to natural pleasures and struggles to enjoy anything outside addictive behaviours. Recovery from addiction entails overcoming this state of emptiness, dullness, and lack of motivation to engage in healthy activities.

Anhedonia during recovery raises the risk of relapse. Without the ability to derive joy from everyday activities, we may turn to addictive substances or behaviours to alleviate emotional distress. A holistic approach to rehabilitation addresses anhedonia by helping to rebuild the brain's reward system. This may involve therapy, support groups, lifestyle changes, and, in some cases, medication or supplements to balance neurotransmitters and manage anhedonia.

DOPAMINE STACKING

Dopamine stacking involves combining multiple activities that release dopamine, creating a temporary feeling of euphoria. However, this practice has hidden costs. Over time, dopamine stacking leads to allostatic load – the cumulative strain on the body and brain from chronic stress. This strain can result in various physical and mental health issues, such as sleep disturbances, mood swings, and reduced cognitive function.

Example of Dopamine Stacking in the Morning

- **Coffee**: Caffeine increases dopamine levels, stimulating alertness.
- **Vaping (Nicotine)**: Nicotine offers a quick dopamine hit.
- **Sugar-based breakfast cereals**: Sugar spikes dopamine through a surge of glucose.
- **Social media scrolling**: Notifications and "likes" offer dopamine through the anticipation of social approval.

This sequence may seem like a perfect way to start the day with energy, but there are significant downsides:

- **Diminished effects**: Over time, the body becomes accustomed to these stimuli, requiring increasingly higher doses to achieve the same dopamine response, leading to a cycle of stacking.
- **Crash and burnout**: Following the dopamine surge, there is a dip in mood and energy, leaving you feeling sluggish and anxious.
- **Health risks**: Each of these activities, from excessive caffeine to sugar intake and nicotine use, carries its own health risks, which are compounded when combined.

A healthier routine might include:

- **Exercise**: Physical activity naturally boosts dopamine levels and provides sustained energy.
- **Meditation**: Mindfulness practices regulate dopamine and improve well-being.
- **Healthy breakfast**: A balanced breakfast with protein and complex carbohydrates provides sustained energy.
- **Social interaction**: Connecting with loved ones in person cultivates genuine social rewards.

- **Intellectual stimulation**: Engaging in activities that challenge the mind promotes positive dopamine responses.
- **Spiritual connection**: Setting intentions, practising gratitude, and focusing on spiritual growth elevate mood and purpose.

True happiness and well-being are built on balanced, sustainable habits, not chasing a quick dopamine fix.

CROSS-ADDICTION EXPLAINED

Cross-addiction occurs when you transition from one addictive behaviour or substance to another. This happens when the brain becomes desensitised to the dopamine release associated with a specific substance or activity, leading you to seek out new sources of dopamine to achieve the same high.

Factors that Contribute to Cross-Addiction

- **Underlying emotional issues**: Unaddressed emotional pain, trauma, or stress can fuel addictive behaviours. The shift from one addiction to another may be an attempt to avoid confronting these deeper issues.
- **Seeking novelty:** The brain is naturally inclined to seek out new and rewarding experiences, which can lead people to switch addictions in search of fresh dopamine hits.
- **Easy accessibility:** Modern life bombards us with constant stimuli that trigger addictive behaviours, from social media to processed foods, making it difficult to resist cravings.

The Risks of Cross-Addiction

- **Substitution, not solution**: Cross-addiction fails to address the root causes of the addiction, perpetuating a cycle of shifting from one dependency to another.

- **Compounded health problems**: Each addiction carries its own set of health risks, and cross-addiction exacerbates these issues, leading to multiple health concerns.
- **Disrupted life**: Cross-addiction can negatively impact work, relationships, finances, and other areas of life.
- **Diminished self-control**: It can erode the ability to resist cravings and make healthy choices.
- **Escalating cycle**: As habituation sets in, you may seek more potent or dangerous sources of dopamine, increasing the potential for harm.

Preventing Cross-Addiction

To prevent cross-addiction, it's essential to address its root causes and develop healthier coping mechanisms, often with the help of professional treatment. Additional strategies include:

- **Trigger identification**: Recognise the situations or emotions that lead to cravings and develop healthy coping strategies.
- **Support system development**: Surround yourself with supportive friends, family, or a professional network to resist cravings.
- **Self-care**: Prioritise adequate sleep, balanced nutrition, regular exercise, and constructive social interactions.

Cross-Addiction: The Slippery Slope from Vaping Nicotine to Alcohol and Food

Nicotine, alcohol, and food can form a dangerous cycle of cross-addiction. Here's how it often unfolds:

1. **Nicotine and Dopamine:** Vaping nicotine releases dopamine, reinforcing the habit and creating dependence.
2. **Quitting Vaping and the Shift:** When quitting vaping, dopamine levels initially drop, leading to anxiety, irritability, and depression.

3. **Seeking New Sources of Pleasure:** The brain craves new sources of dopamine, often turning to food (especially high-sugar or high-fat foods) or alcohol to fill the void.

This cycle can escalate:

- **Increased food intake**: Compensating for the lack of dopamine from nicotine by overeating.
- **Alcohol as a substitute**: Turning to alcohol for relaxation and mood elevation.

As the cycle continues, overeating and increased alcohol consumption can lead to weight gain, health problems, and potentially even new addictions.

Why People Eat More After Quitting Vaping

- **Oral fixation**: Smoking involves a physical sensation of holding and manipulating something. When quitting, some people replace this with food.
- **Metabolic changes**: Nicotine affects metabolism, and quitting may slightly lower metabolic rate, causing feelings of hunger.
- **Emotional eating**: The stress and anxiety from quitting vaping may trigger emotional eating.

BREAKING THE CYCLE

To address cross-addiction and develop healthier habits, consider the following:

- **Identify triggers**: Recognise what prompts cravings for nicotine, alcohol, or unhealthy foods and plan alternative coping strategies.
- **Seek support**: Join a support group or find a life coach or therapist to help you navigate quitting smoking and developing healthy coping mechanisms.

- **Focus on healthy dopamine boosters**: Exercise, meditation, time in nature, and engaging in enjoyable hobbies can naturally increase dopamine levels and enhance mood.

By understanding the risks of cross-addiction and taking proactive steps, you can successfully break free from unhealthy cycles and build a healthier, more balanced lifestyle.

DOPAMINE DELUGE: HOW SMARTPHONES HIJACK OUR BRAINS

Dr Anna Lembke's insights shed light on the problematic impact that smartphones have on our dopamine systems, raising concerns about their addictive potential. She compares smartphones to hypodermic needles, highlighting their ability to deliver instant gratification and excitement. These devices offer us immediate access to a world filled with stimulating experiences, presented on lively screens that enhance their appeal and compel us to keep coming back for more.

THE DOPAMINE TRAP

Smartphone apps, on-screen games, and social media platforms are deliberately designed to trigger impulsive behaviours. Users can endlessly scroll through feeds, share updates, or interact with content, receiving instant rewards in the form of likes, comments, or rankings. Social media taps into our fundamental need for connection and validation by offering a constant stream of positive reinforcement. This rapid feedback loop fuels addictive behaviours. Social media giants like Facebook, Instagram, and YouTube excel at manipulating the dopamine system, bombarding users with fresh content, messages, and social interactions. This continuous cycle keeps users engaged and heightens their desire for more rewards.

Beyond Dr Lembke's observations, the addictive nature of technology also exploits our inherent vulnerabilities. This feedback loop strengthens our dependency on social media, making it harder to detach. Furthermore, smartphones exploit our natural inclination to seek novelty, constantly enticing us with new experiences that further deepen our engagement.

Beyond the Screen

Excessive reliance on technology can lead to withdrawal symptoms – including discomfort and irritability – when separated from devices, social media, or on-screen games. The craving for the dopamine release these activities provide compels us to return to our screens. Over time, prolonged technology use dulls the brain's reward system, reducing the enjoyment derived from real-world activities, which often seem pale in comparison to the immediate pleasures offered by smartphones. Dr Lembke emphasises the importance of mindful and balanced technology use to maintain a healthy connection with both the digital world and the tangible one.

TIPS FOR TECH MINDFULNESS

Being aware of the addictive nature of smartphones and technology is imperative. By understanding their mechanisms, you can adopt a more mindful and balanced approach to your digital consumption. Here are a few strategies:

- **Set Boundaries**: Establish daily smartphone usage limits and stick to them.
- **Detox from Social Media**: Be mindful of how social media affects you. Take regular breaks if it triggers negative emotions.
- **Embrace Real Life:** Prioritise activities that don't involve your smartphone, such as spending time with loved ones, exercising, or reading a book.

Dearest Fellow Traveller,

The story of the monkeys in India, drawn into captivity by the allure of a seemingly harmless banana, holds a profound truth that resonates with us all. It speaks to the powerful grip of unhealthy attachments – to substances, behaviours, or patterns that, at first, offer comfort, pleasure, or escape. Yet, like the tempting banana, these initial comforts can quickly transform into traps, entangling us in a web of negative consequences that spread through every corner of our lives.

Why do we hold on so tightly, even when we know we're caught in a trap of our own making? The answer lies in the intricate dance of dopamine release, the fear of the unknown, the deceptive comfort of the familiar, and the powerful force of habit. But unlike the caged monkeys, we possess the key to our own freedom. It is not hidden in the grasp of a deceptive banana but within us – in the wellspring of resilience that is waiting to be unlocked.

This journey toward freedom may seem daunting, but rest assured, you are not alone. By reaching out for support, seeking professional guidance, and embracing healthier sources of dopamine, you can begin to loosen the grip of addiction and step onto a transformative path. Picture the strength you will uncover, the self-compassion that will grow, and the life filled with meaning and fulfilment that awaits you on the other side.

Take a deep breath, fellow Wayfinder. Open your hand to the possibility of a brighter future. The support you seek is here, and the path to freedom is well within your reach.

With hope and encouragement,

Vincenzia

CHAPTER 3 SUMMARY

THE PLEASURE PRINCIPLE AND PAIN AVOIDANCE

Human behaviour is driven by the pursuit of pleasure and avoidance of pain, regulated by dopamine.

Dopamine reinforces rewarding behaviours, but dysregulation leads to addictive patterns.

ADDICTION AND THE DOPAMINE CYCLE

Addiction starts with dopamine surges from substances or behaviours, creating dependency and diminishing natural rewards. Over time, tolerance develops, driving the need for higher doses or repeated behaviours.

BREAKING FREE

Recovery requires understanding addiction's neurobiology and addressing it through therapy, mindfulness, and support systems. Self-compassion and healthy habits help recalibrate dopamine balance and restore well-being.

THE ILLUSION OF THE "ALMOST"

Addiction masks deeper issues, trapping us in cycles of temporary relief without true resolution.

Recognising this illusion is key to embracing sustainable change and authentic fulfilment.

HEALTHY DOPAMINE SOURCES

Activities like exercise, mindfulness, learning, and acts of kindness promote natural dopamine production. Avoid quick fixes and focus on long-term fulfilment through balanced, health-promoting behaviours.

NEURAL PATHWAYS IN ADDICTION

Addiction creates entrenched neural loops of cravings and reinforcement. Strengthened pathways amplify cravings, reduce control, and lead to severe personal consequences.

BALANCING PLEASURE AND PAIN

The brain seeks a balance between pleasure and pain – addiction disrupts this equilibrium, leading to tolerance and withdrawal. Recovery restores homeostasis, emphasising genuine satisfaction over fleeting highs.

CROSS-ADDICTION AND ANHEDONIA

Addiction can shift between substances or behaviours, perpetuating dependency. Anhedonia, or the inability to feel joy, often accompanies recovery and requires intentional efforts to rebuild natural reward systems.

DOPAMINE AND TECHNOLOGY

Smartphones exploit dopamine pathways, creating dependency and reducing satisfaction from natural rewards. Mindful tech use and intentional breaks can restore balance.

PREVENTING AND MANAGING ADDICTION

Address triggers and underlying issues with therapy, support networks, and healthy coping mechanisms. Holistic strategies like sleep, nutrition, and creative expression support sustainable recovery.

REFLECTIVE PROMPTS

Here are some prompts to help you explore how dopamine-seeking behaviours have shaped your life.

- Personal Connection: Reflect on a time when you sought pleasure or avoided pain through a particular behaviour. How did it affect your life in the short term and long term?
- Understanding Triggers: Identify any substances or behaviours in your life that may create a dopamine "rush". How do they influence your actions and emotions?
- The "Almost" Illusion: Think about situations where you have chased the "almost" solution. How did it impact your well-being, and what could you have done differently?
- Balancing Pleasure and Pain: Consider how the pursuit of pleasure and avoidance of pain shape your daily decisions. Are there areas where this balance feels off?
- Dopamine and Connection: Reflect on how your relationships, social interactions, or use of technology influence your dopamine levels. Do they enhance or disrupt your sense of fulfilment?
- Recovery and Resilience: If you've experienced addiction or dependency, what steps have you taken (or could you take) to recalibrate your brain's dopamine balance?
- Healthy Coping Strategies: Explore which health-promoting behaviours – like exercise, mindfulness, or creative pursuits – you could incorporate to naturally boost dopamine.
- Technology's Grip: How does your smartphone or other technology impact your mental health and dopamine regulation? Could you benefit from implementing tech mindfulness practices?
- The Cycle of Addiction: Reflect on any repetitive behaviours or habits that may indicate a problematic reinforcement loop in your life. How might you break free from this cycle?
- Finding Fulfilment: Consider what activities or practices bring you long-term satisfaction and joy. How can you prioritise these over fleeting dopamine "highs"?

REFLECTION PROMPTS FOR HEALTHCARE WORKERS, COUNSELLORS AND COACHES

This exploration of addiction through the lens of dopamine is crucial - Here are some prompts to deepen your understanding and enhance your approach:

SELF-AWARENESS AND REFLECTION

- **Your Dopamine Lens:** Reflect on your own habits and activities. Are there any that trigger excessive dopamine release, potentially hindering your ability to be fully present for your clients?
- **Understanding "Almost":** Recall a situation where a client expressed the "almost worked" sentiment about their negative behaviour. How did you guide them to explore the limitations of this approach and identify healthier alternatives?

ENHANCING COACHING AND COUNSELLING TECHNIQUES

- **Cravings Navigation**: How can you effectively explain the science behind cravings and empower your clients to manage them constructively?
- **Balancing Act Exploration**: How can you facilitate discussions about the delicate balance between pleasure and pain? How can you encourage clients to prioritise natural rewards and delayed gratification?
- **Cross-Addiction Awareness**: Be mindful of the potential for cross-addictions (switching addictions). How can you screen for and address this issue during the coaching/counselling process?

OPTIMISING YOUR CLIENT SUPPORT

- **Beyond Techniques**: While techniques play a role, how can you integrate a more holistic approach, incorporating practices like mindfulness and nurturing strong social connections to support healthy dopamine regulation in your clients?
- **The Tech Talk**: How can you initiate open conversations with clients about their technology use and its potential impact on their dopamine systems?

- **Relapse as a Process**: How can you help clients understand and navigate relapse not as a failure but as a natural part of the recovery journey?

CONTINUOUS LEARNING AND GROWTH

- **Staying Updated**: Addiction research is constantly evolving. How can you remain current on the latest discoveries related to dopamine and its role in motivation and reward?
- **Building Your Resilience**: Compassion fatigue can be a challenge. How can you prioritise your own well-being to build resilience and continue providing effective support?
- **Community Advocacy**: Consider the social and environmental factors that contribute to addiction. How can you advocate for policies and resources that promote overall community health and well-being?

RESOURCES

BOOKS

- ***Dopamine Nation: Finding Balance in the Age of Indulgence*** by Dr Anna Lembke – Explores dopamine's role in addiction.
- ***The Biology of Desire: Why Addiction Is Not a Disease*** by Marc Lewis – Challenges traditional addiction views, focusing on neuroscience.
- ***The Craving Mind*** by Judson Brewer – Examines mindfulness in addiction recovery.
- ***The Miracle of Mindfulness*** by Thich Nhat Hanh – Offers techniques for incorporating mindfulness into daily life.
- ***Radical Acceptance*** by Tara Brach – Combines Buddhist wisdom and Western psychology, emphasising self-compassion.
- ***Buddha's Brain*** by Rick Hanson – Blends neuroscience with Buddhist principles for happiness and well-being. TED talk.

DOCUMENTARY

The Social Dilemma – Explores the addictive nature of technology and social media.

YOUTUBE CHANNELS AND PODCASTS

- **AsapSCIENCE Link** – Offers engaging content on brain science and addiction.
- **PsychedSubstance** – Explores substance use and its brain effects.
- **Recovery Elevator Podcast** – Discusses addiction and recovery, with a focus on dopamine and cravings.
- **The Craving Brain Podcast** – Delves into addiction science, cravings, and recovery.

CHAPTER 4 - THE HEALING POWER OF CONNECTION

FINDING SOLACE IN CONNECTION

Maya wandered the winding streets of the neighbourhood she'd lived in since childhood. Her steps were aimless, with no clear direction. This state had become her new normal. Every person who passed her, with heads lowered and gazes averted, felt like just another door shutting in her face. The laughter of a child behind her cruelly reminded her of the familial connection she so desperately craved but always felt was beyond her reach.

The shadows of her troubled childhood loomed large, their impact lingering in every empty wine bottle cluttering her kitchen counter. Wine had become her solitary refuge, a temporary escape from the ache in her heart. Yet, unfortunately, it guided her deeper into a maze of confusion and isolation. Addiction drowned all connection and belonging and gradually built a stronghold of isolation.

One blustery autumn evening, the swirling leaves – a promise of change – went unnoticed, and Maya was once again caught in the prison of her thoughts. Shades of amber, crimson, ochre, and burnished gold swirled through the wind, each leaf surrendering to the inevitable with quiet courage. Totally defeated, she sat down on the sidewalk. She looked up and noticed an unfamiliar sign on the pavement on the opposite side of the street. Unlike the usual advertisements, stark reminders of the life she wasn't living, this one held a simple, poignant message written in elegant, bold letters:

Compassionate Recovery: Embrace Hope & Healing. All welcome!

Curiosity tugged at the corners of her mind, nudging her out of her funk. The warmth of those words seeped through the evening's chill, igniting a faint flicker of hope amidst her lingering despair. With a deep breath, she stood up, her mind wrestling with the weight of apprehension. She crossed the street and gazed at the door in front of her, feeling both invited and intimidated. The promise of possibility was tempered with a sense of fear and uncertainty.

Finally, her trembling hand pushed open the door. She stepped into the warmth, where a group of strangers sat chatting around a coffee table. In an attempt to avert eye contact, she started scanning the bookshelves resting heavily against the surrounding walls. They were brimming with well-used books on various topics of recovery, healing, and transformation. Maya, hesitantly and as inconspicuously as possible, took a seat.

THE POWER OF SHARED EXPERIENCES

Over the following weeks, Maya returned to read the books on the shelves that she resonated with. She also joined their compassionate recovery group, where she listened to stories told with raw honesty. Each tale was an unvarnished account of pain, resilience, and the longing for redemption. Their words wove together a landscape of vulnerability and strength, and in time, something started to shift within her. The weight of her own story began to lighten.

In this humble space, Maya began to chip away at the layers of her personal suffering. The fortress of isolation she had so carefully constructed began to crumble. She began to realise that she wasn't an island shrouded in fog but part of a vast, interconnected archipelago of shared human experience. Tears of incredible relief welled in her eyes. For the first time, she felt a spark of belonging. Her story, once a solitary burden, became a thread in the larger narrative of resilience and hope shared by those around her.

THE SEASONS OF TRANSFORMATION

The power of connection fuelled Maya's recovery journey, as mirrored by the changing seasons around her. Winter faded away as spring unfolded, and delicate blossoms emerged from the bare branches that lined her neighbourhood's streets. These transformations reflected the renewal within Maya's soul. No longer did she seek solace in the depths of a bottle – instead, she embraced the unwavering support of her newfound community. Their presence provided the stability she needed amidst the unpredictable winds of life. Vulnerability, once one of her greatest fears, became her pivotal strength.

THE ANTIDOTE TO ADDICTION

Through this journey, Maya unearthed a crucial truth: the opposite of addiction is connection. We find it in our shared humanity and the steady rhythm of empathy and self-compassion. Addiction had thrived in her self-imposed isolation, feeding on her belief that she was unworthy of love and belonging. But the group shattered this illusion, reminding her that healing happens through acceptance, understanding, and a supportive community.

As she stepped deeper into her recovery, Maya discovered the transformative integration of the four pillars of healing: belonging, joy, freedom, and love. These pillars became her guiding light, helping her navigate the shadows of her past and embrace a future filled with promise. Within the warmth of her community, she found not just hope but the courage to reclaim her life.

A SACRED SPACE FOR WHOLENESS

Maya's journey stands as a testament to the healing power of connection. In the sacred embrace of this group, she found more than just support - she found herself. Here, amidst understanding hearts, she began to rebuild – not alone but surrounded by those who understood the weight of her struggles and the beauty of her resilience. Together, they forged unbreakable bonds, transforming pain into purpose and isolation into belonging.

As Maya walked forward on her path to wholeness, she carried with her the important knowledge that no one heals alone. Connection had not only saved her but had opened the door to a life enriched with meaning, authenticity, and love. It was here, in the shared stories and compassionate presence of others, that Maya discovered the truest form of solace: the healing power of connection.

THE FOUR PILLARS OF RECOVERY: A FOUNDATION FOR WHOLENESS

The journey of addiction recovery is complex and deeply personal, requiring a holistic approach that addresses the mind, body, and spirit. At the heart of this transformative process are the four pillars of recovery – belonging, joy, freedom, and love – which provide a sturdy foundation for healing and sustained growth.

BELONGING: THE ANCHOR OF CONNECTION

Belonging is a fundamental human need and a crucial part of recovery. It begins with nurturing healthy connections, both internally and externally. This combats the isolation that fuels addiction.

Key Aspects of Belonging

- **Self-connection**: Embracing self-acceptance by honouring your unique values, emotions, and experiences.
- **Community**: Building supportive relationships with others who understand and empathise with your journey.
- **Connection to the world**: Engaging in activities that create purpose, such as spending time in nature, volunteering, or pursuing creative outlets.

JOY: CULTIVATING INNER LIGHT

Joy is a powerful source of strength in recovery, emanating from within rather than depending on external circumstances. It serves as a reminder of life's beauty and the resilience within you.

Ways to Cultivate Joy

- **Healthy attachments**: Invest in relationships that bring positivity and fulfilment.
- **Savouring life**: Focus on small pleasures, like the warmth of sunlight or the taste of a favourite meal.
- **Personal growth**: Celebrate each milestone in your recovery journey, however small, as a victory.

FREEDOM: RECLAIMING YOUR POWER

Freedom is about breaking free from the chains of addiction and rediscovering your authentic self. It empowers you to take control of your life and live in alignment with your deepest values.

Steps Toward Freedom:

- **Reclaim your authentic self**: Reflect on your aspirations and rediscover the person you want to be.
- **Live with integrity**: Make choices that reflect your values, even when faced with challenges.
- **Break unhealthy patterns**: Identify and replace behaviours tied to addiction with healthier habits.

LOVE: THE HEART OF TRANSFORMATION

Love is the binding force in recovery, encompassing compassion for yourself and others. It provides the emotional sustenance needed for transformation and sustained growth.

How to Express Love:

- **Self-love**: Develop self-compassion by treating yourself with kindness and understanding, even in moments of struggle.
- **Love for others**: Build and nurture relationships with those who support your healing.
- **Giving love**: Share kindness and compassion with others, nurturing mutual growth and connection.

PRACTICAL TOOLS FOR BUILDING YOUR FOUR PILLARS OF RECOVERY

Recovery includes rebuilding a life rooted in connection, joy, the freedom of personal empowerment, and love. These Four Pillars of Recovery provide a foundation for lasting change, helping you cultivate a meaningful and fulfilling life. By strengthening each pillar with practical tools and intentional actions, you create a resilient support system for yourself, ensuring that your recovery is not just about surviving but thriving.

Below, you'll find actionable steps to reinforce these pillars, guiding you toward a life of belonging, joy, freedom, and love.

BELONGING: BUILDING CONNECTIONS

Recovery flourishes in connection. A strong support system helps combat isolation and promotes a sense of belonging. By actively engaging in supportive relationships, you create a network of encouragement and understanding that sustains your healing journey.

- **Support Groups and Therapy:** Join a recovery group or seek therapy to cultivate healthier relationships and combat isolation.
- **Volunteering**: Find purpose and community by giving back to others.

JOY: CULTIVATING INNER HAPPINESS

True recovery includes rediscovering joy. By nurturing gratitude, presence, and passion, you can shift from merely existing to truly living. Cultivating joy brings lightness and fulfilment to your path.

- **Gratitude Practice**: Keep a gratitude journal to reflect on and appreciate life's simple joys.
- **Mindfulness Meditation**: Stay present in the moment and savour your experiences.
- **Engaging in Hobbies**: Rediscover or explore activities that bring you joy and fulfilment.

FREEDOM: RECLAIMING YOUR POWER

Healing is an act of reclaiming agency over your life. Recognising triggers, setting boundaries, and making intentional choices empower you to break free from old patterns and create a future aligned with your values and aspirations.

- **Mindfulness of Triggers**: Develop awareness of your triggers and implement strategies to manage them.
- **Setting Boundaries**: Learn to say no and protect your values and well-being.
- **Decision-Making Tools**: Use techniques like pros-and-cons lists or journaling to align decisions with your goals and values.

LOVE: NURTURING SELF-COMPASSION AND CONNECTION

At the heart of recovery is love - both for yourself and others. By practising self-compassion, nurturing meaningful relationships, and extending kindness, you cultivate a life of deeper connection and purpose.

- **Self-Compassion Practices**: Incorporate daily affirmations and self-care routines to cultivate inner kindness.
- **Building Support Networks**: Surround yourself with empathetic people who uplift and encourage you.
- **Random Acts of Kindness**: Practice small acts of generosity to deepen your connections and nurture a sense of purpose.

THE POWER OF THE FOUR PILLARS

These four pillars are not static destinations but evolving practices that will support your recovery journey. As you cultivate each pillar, you'll discover the interconnectedness between them. Belonging fuels joy, joy reinforces freedom, and freedom deepens love. Together, they provide a holistic framework for healing, resilience, and the rediscovery of a life worth living.

BEYOND ISOLATION: THE CRUCIAL ROLE OF CONNECTION IN ADDICTION RECOVERY

For decades, addiction was viewed through a narrow lens, focusing almost exclusively on the chemical properties of substances. However, recent research and lived experiences reveal a more nuanced reality: social connection and environmental factors play a pivotal role in both the development of and recovery from addiction. These insights call for a compassionate, holistic approach to recovery that addresses the profound human need for connection.

THE SCIENCE OF CONNECTION AND ADDICTION

THE RAT PARK EXPERIMENT

Conventional addiction studies placed isolated rats in cages with access to drug-laced water, consistently showing high levels of consumption. However, the ground-breaking Rat Park experiment challenged this paradigm. Researchers created an enriched environment where rats enjoyed social interaction, ample space, and engaging activities. The findings were remarkable: rats in enriched environments consumed significantly less drug-laced water than those in isolation. This experiment brings into focus the critical role of social connection and environmental stimulation in mitigating addiction.

HUMAN EVIDENCE: THE VIETNAM HEROIN ADDICTION PARADOX

The Vietnam War presented an unintentional, real-world experiment in addiction. Many U.S. soldiers developed heroin dependencies during their deployment. Conventional wisdom predicted widespread addiction upon their return. Instead, the majority overcame their dependence without traditional treatment. Johann Hari, in his book Chasing the Scream, highlights that soldiers with strong social connections and supportive environments transitioned back into fulfilling lives, demonstrating the profound impact of reintegration and belonging.

THE TRANSFORMATIVE POWER OF CONNECTION IN RECOVERY

Connection is more than a luxury – it's a fundamental human need and an integral part of recovery. Here's how nurturing connection can transform the recovery journey:

- **Belonging and Community**: Combat the isolation of addiction with shared experiences, mutual acceptance, and a sense of being part of something larger.
- **Support and Encouragement**: Gain strength and motivation from peers who understand the challenges of recovery.
- **Emotional Validation**: Feeling seen, heard, and understood reduces loneliness and creates healthy emotional expression.
- **Safe Spaces**: Open discussions in judgement-free environments help one confront challenges with honesty.
- **Healthy Coping Mechanisms**: Learn and practice constructive ways to manage stress and emotions.

- **Purpose and Meaning**: Rebuild a life filled with fulfilment and direction, moving beyond the shadow of addiction.

NURTURING CONNECTION: PRACTICAL STRATEGIES

HEALTHY SOCIAL INTERACTION

- **Sober Social Events:** Attend movie nights, game nights, or outings organised by support groups to form bonds in substance-free settings.
- **Peer Support Networks**: Join sober living communities or online forums to nurture mutual accountability and understanding.

ENVIRONMENTAL STIMULATION

- **Art Therapy**: Participate in workshops or classes to express emotions creatively while connecting with others in a supportive setting.
- **Adventure Therapy**: Engage in activities like rock climbing or hiking to build teamwork skills, personal growth, and a connection to nature.
- **Therapeutic Gardens**: Volunteer or participate in gardening programs to enjoy sensory stimulation, relaxation, and a connection with the environment.

FULFILLING ACTIVITIES

- **Vocational Training**: Enrol in programs to build skills, enhance self-esteem, and create opportunities for personal and professional growth.
- **Music Therapy**: Try songwriting, playing instruments, or singing to promote emotional expression and forge social bonds.
- **Outdoor Recreation**: Pursue activities like gardening, fishing, or camping to improve physical health, find relaxation, and connect with nature.

EMBRACING THE MUD: BECOMING THE LOTUS

In the tranquil embrace of a serene pond, where subaqueous chaos dances with beauty, the lotus emerges as a symbol of purity, resilience, and awakening. Beneath the calm surface lies a hidden world of tangled vines rooted in the mire of the mud. As dawn breaks, a diligent gardener gently navigates the serene waters, surrounded by thick vines, giant emerald leaves, and cloudy water, careful not to disturb the foundation or uproot the plants. His skilled hands caress the petals of a single lotus flower at its peak of perfection and pluck it. The gardener gifts this delicate lotus flower to the monks at his monastery to place at the altar — not just as an offering but as a silent prayer.

The lotus, in its awe-inspiring grace, transcends mere existence, becoming a symbol of triumph – emerging from the depths, growing relentlessly amidst murky waters towards the sunlit shallows, and eventually birthing into beauty and purity. Similar to the lotus emerging from the pond's mire, our journey of growth reflects this ascent, emerging from the soil of life's challenges and hardships.

Life, with its complex twists and turns, can resemble a muddy pond. Yet, if we dare to engage with it fully, navigating its ebbs and flows, each stumble, each fall, each encounter with hardship – these challenges can sculpt a path of unforeseen splendour. It is in moments of struggle and discomfort that our true resilience is refined. Picture a modest seed nestled in the gloomy, damp depths of the pond. Here, amid the obscurity, the seed begins its brave quest toward the light. It extends delicate tendrils, reaching out for nourishment and growth, drawing sustenance from the very mud that surrounds it.

Similarly, we must learn to embrace life's dark and often challenging moments. Just as the lotus cannot bloom without the nourishment of the mud, we cannot truly thrive without confronting the trials life presents. Let us tend to the murky depths with care, like the gardeners, ensuring that the seed within us has the opportunity to reach the light and unfurl into its full magnificence. Like the lotus unfolding its petals to the morning sun, we, too, can find tranquillity and grace amidst life's most arduous circumstances.

As we journey through the gardens of life, let us heed the wisdom of the lotus: from darkness emerges light, from struggle arises strength, and murkiness is transformed into splendour. Embrace the muck, for it is the very substance upon which your journey to the lotus is founded. Embrace the mire, for it serves as a stepping stone on your voyage to personal transformation and enlightenment.

Dear traveller, when you find yourself ensnared in life's challenges, remember the story of the lotus.

The book "No Mud, No Lotus" by Thich Nhat Hanh served as inspiration for this piece of writing.

THE DOMINO EFFECT: TRAUMA, ADDICTION RECOVERY, AND PERSONAL GROWTH

The intricate interplay among trauma, addiction recovery, and personal growth creates a complex and multifaceted chain reaction. Literature often provides a powerful lens through which to examine this dynamic relationship. In the story "Embracing the Mud", the evocative metaphor of the lotus flower and the muddy pond illustrates this very connection. The murky pond represents the emotional turmoil and pain associated with trauma, which can push someone into the muddy depths of addiction just as the lotus begins its life in the mud. However, the beauty of the lotus unfolding its petals symbolises the potential for personal growth and transformation that arises from overcoming these challenges.

This connection between trauma and addiction recovery is also illustrated in Maya's story. Maya's childhood trauma fuels her dependence on alcohol, creating a sense of isolation and distancing her from the connections she desperately craves. However, stepping into a support group becomes a pivotal moment, introducing her to the four pillars of recovery: belonging, joy, freedom, and love. These pillars guide her journey, promoting connection and offering the tools to cultivate self-love and rebuild her life.

Understanding the link between trauma, addiction recovery, and personal growth is imperative. While trauma can steer someone down the path of addiction, the journey of recovery offers a powerful opportunity for transformation. By encouraging connections, embracing joy, reclaiming freedom, and cultivating self-love, it's possible to break free from the shackles of the past and bloom into one's full potential, much like the lotus rising from the mud.

REBUILDING WHOLENESS: SIX CORE ELEMENTS OF COMPASSIONATE RECOVERY

Compassionate recovery is a multifaceted journey that aims to reconnect you to a state of wholeness and well-being. This process requires dedication and self-compassion, but it ultimately empowers you to reclaim your life. The journey is built upon six key pillars, each playing a vital role in achieving successful recovery.

1. **Reconnecting with Your Authentic Self**: Recovery begins by peeling back the layers of self-deception to rediscover your true essence. This is your authentic self, free from the influence of addiction. It's about unearthing your core values, strengths, and passions. By reconnecting with your authentic self, you rediscover who you are at your core and what truly matters to you.

2. **Reconnecting with and Healing Your Body**: Compassionate recovery places priority on physical health. Addressing any underlying medical conditions related to addiction or mental health is essential. This also involves adopting healthy lifestyle habits such as proper nutrition, regular exercise, and adequate sleep. A healthy body forms the foundation for a healthy mind and spirit. Nourishing your body through these practices strengthens your overall well-being and equips you to face challenges with greater resilience.

3. **Reconnecting with Healthy Thinking**: The mind plays a critical role in the recovery process. It's important to confront and challenge the negative thought patterns linked to addiction or mental health struggles. By developing cognitive flexibility and adopting healthy coping mechanisms, you can replace negativity with positive self-talk and navigate life's challenges with greater clarity and resilience. Reframing negative thoughts and fostering healthy coping strategies empower you to manage difficult emotions and make constructive choices.

4. **Reconnecting with Your Emotions**: During active addiction, we disconnect from our emotions. Compassionate recovery emphasises the importance of acknowledging, expressing, and regulating your emotions in a healthy way. Through self-awareness and emotional intelligence, you can cultivate resilience and facilitate genuine healing. Learning to manage emotions effectively allows you to navigate life's ups and downs with greater balance and control.

5. **Building Strong Connections**: Strong, supportive relationships are crucial for long-term recovery. This pillar encourages cultivating healthy connections with others, including family, friends, and support groups. These relationships provide a sense of belonging, understanding, and encouragement, serving as a safety net as you navigate the ups and downs of recovery.

6. **Reconnecting with Meaning and Purpose**: Recovery is about more than just surviving – it's about thriving. This pillar focuses on exploring your values and aspirations and creating a path that feels meaningful and fulfilling. For many, this may involve cultivating a spiritual practice or discovering new passions that provide a sense of purpose and connection to something larger than oneself. By reconnecting with what motivates and inspires you, you can build a life that is meaningful and brings joy.

HOW COGNITIVE DISTORTIONS CREATE DISCONNECTIONS IN ADDICTION RECOVERY

Cognitive distortions are patterns of negative thinking that create disconnection and complicate the journey of addiction recovery. These distorted thought patterns lead to unrealistic, irrational, and unhelpful influences that hinder progress. By distorting perceptions and skewing interpretations, these cognitive distortions deepen feelings of disconnection, clouding judgement and impairing rational decision-making.

Common cognitive distortions often emerge in addiction recovery, including:

- **All-or-nothing thinking**: This distortion forces a binary perspective on life devoid of nuance or flexibility. In addiction recovery, it may manifest as seeing any misstep as a catastrophic failure, which undermines confidence, resilience, and the ability to make progress.

- **Overgeneralisation**: Drawing broad conclusions from isolated incidents, this distortion leads to negative self-perception. A single setback may be viewed as an inevitable pattern of failure, damaging motivation and hope for the future.
- **Mental filtering**: This involves tunnel vision focused on the negative, eclipsing any positive aspects of recovery. By magnifying setbacks and dismissing progress, it creates a sense of futility and despair.
- **Discounting the positive**: Minimising achievements or milestones diminishes self-worth and impedes confidence. This distortion perpetuates a cycle of self-doubt, undermining belief in one's capacity for change.
- **Jumping to conclusions**: Assuming negative judgements from others fuels paranoia and self-criticism, creating cycles of shame and anxiety that reinforce maladaptive coping mechanisms.

These cognitive distortions not only cloud judgement but also amplify negative emotions like shame, guilt, and hopelessness, increasing the likelihood of relapse and perpetuating the cycle of addiction.

Addressing these distortions is essential in addiction treatment. Cognitive-behavioural therapy (CBT) and Dialectical Behaviour Therapy (DBT) are effective tools for challenging and reframing these unhelpful thought patterns. By developing awareness and practising cognitive restructuring, you can cultivate healthier, more rational perspectives, enhancing resilience and fostering sustainable recovery.

One practical strategy for confronting cognitive distortions is to assess the validity and utility of your thoughts. For instance, asking questions such as "Is this thought realistic?" or "Is this thought helpful?" can help break the grip of distorted thinking. For example, challenging the thought "I'm a failure because of one mistake" can lead to reflection on personal growth and a more balanced perspective, enabling you to view setbacks in a healthier light.

By confronting and reframing cognitive distortions, you can build pathways to clarity, resilience, and authentic connection in your journey toward lasting recovery.

SOBRIETY VS. RECOVERY: UNDERSTANDING THE DISTINCTION

Though often used interchangeably, sobriety and recovery hold distinct meanings.

Sobriety refers to the absence of substance use or addictive behaviours. It marks a significant milestone, demonstrating a commitment to abstaining from harmful substances. However, sobriety primarily addresses the symptoms of addiction without necessarily exploring the deeper causes.

Recovery, on the other hand, is a comprehensive, transformative process that goes beyond mere abstinence. It involves holistic healing, addressing both the symptoms and underlying causes of addiction and mental health struggles. Key features of recovery include:

- A recovery involves exploring and processing past traumas, identifying triggers, and building self-awareness to promote lasting change.
- A recovery equips you with practical tools for navigating challenges, such as stress management techniques, communication skills, and resilience-building.
- A recovery encourages you to discover and create a fulfilling life, including identifying passions, setting goals, and building a strong support network.

In essence:

- **Sobriety** is an important initial step in the recovery journey.
- **Recovery** is a sustained, multi-faceted process that builds upon sobriety.

Understanding this distinction empowers you to approach healing holistically, addressing both the symptoms and root causes of addiction. While sobriety is crucial, recovery is characterised by ongoing growth, self-discovery, and transformation. In recovery, you may encounter challenges like managing emotions, navigating relationships, and finding purpose in life. However, by embracing these challenges as opportunities for growth, you can continue to progress on the path to holistic wellness.

THE TRANSFORMATIVE POWER OF RECOVERY: RENEWAL AND GROWTH

Recovery from addiction is not just about stopping harmful behaviours – it's a transformative journey of self-discovery, renewal, healing, and growth. This journey leads to a life of authenticity, fulfilment, and connection. Here are key aspects of the transformative power of recovery:

- **Rediscovering Your Authentic Self**: Addiction can conceal your true identity beneath layers of coping mechanisms and distorted self-perception. Recovery empowers you to peel back these layers, reconnecting with your authentic self, free from the influence of addiction.
- **Finding Meaning and Purpose**: Addiction often offers a temporary escape, but recovery encourages you to seek genuine meaning and purpose. It encourages the exploration of activities aligned with your true self, enabling you to discover passions, relationships, and aspirations that bring lasting fulfilment.
- **Unveiling Your Inner Landscape**: Recovery is a profound journey of self-discovery. By exploring the roots of addiction, understanding triggers and vulnerabilities, and cultivating self-awareness, you can build resilience and foster lasting change.
- **Healing from Trauma**: Trauma is typically a significant contributor to addiction. Recovery creates a safe space for confronting and healing from past traumas, releasing their lingering impact.

- **Embracing Self-Acceptance**: In recovery, you learn to embrace self-acceptance, letting go of shame and judgement. This process involves recognising your inherent worth and embracing compassion for yourself, regardless of past struggles.
- **Cultivating Growth**: Recovery is an ongoing process of personal growth. You'll learn to navigate life's challenges, develop resilience, and acquire coping skills that improve all aspects of your life – not just your recovery.
- **Reconnecting with Others**: Addiction often leads to isolation and broken relationships. Recovery offers the opportunity to mend bonds, rebuild trust, and forge authentic connections with loved ones, creating a sense of belonging and support.
- **Living a Balanced Life**: Recovery encourages balance and sustainability. It promotes practices like self-care, moderation, and holistic well-being, helping you create harmony in your personal and social life.
- **Contributing to the Community**: As you progress in your recovery, you may find purpose in helping others facing similar challenges. Through mentorship, advocacy, or peer support, you can contribute to the recovery community, finding fulfilment and meaning in the process.

An Insert from My Journal: The Power of Connection

Dearest me,

Look at you, bravely stepping onto this courageous path of healing. Remember, this journey is carved with your own strength. Though it may stretch into the unknown, know that every step forward brings you closer to wholeness. There will be days when the weight of your past feels like a heavy cloak trying to pull you down. And that's okay. Feel the pain and acknowledge its presence, but don't let it define you. You are so much more than your struggles – you are blooming through adversity like a lotus pushing through the mire.

As you continue to shed the masks and façades, remember that your authentic self is a treasure waiting to be uncovered. Embrace your quirks, passions, dreams, and even the parts you deem "imperfect". Your unwavering determination, your infectious laughter, and even your deepest insecurities – each of these pieces form the vibrant mosaic of your life, more beautiful because of its rich variety.

Above all, never underestimate the healing power of connection. It's in the shared moments with others, the collective acknowledgement of pain, and the quiet understanding in their eyes that you'll find the strength to move forward. Connection reminds us that we are never truly alone. It breaks down walls, softens the edges of isolation, and allows the light of others to guide us when we feel lost. Let this truth anchor you when feelings of doubt and disbelief arise.

You are not just walking this path alone – you are part of a vast web of shared humanity. Your pain is understood, your story is valued, and your presence matters. Reaching out isn't a sign of weakness – it's a sign of courage. By building meaningful connections, you'll find not only solace but also a renewed sense of purpose.

There will be moments of doubt, whispers from the past trying to pull you back. In those moments, hold tight to the strength you've already discovered. Look back on how far you've come and all the battles you've already won. Remember the spark that shines within you, even when it's hidden by shadows.

Your heart is the one that sets the pace for this journey, and this journey is uniquely yours. Celebrate your victories – big and small – and find peace in the quiet moments of growth. You are worthy of healing, love, and happiness. Never forget that. And always remember: the opposite of addiction is not simply sobriety – it's connection.

With unwavering belief and endless love,

Yours truly,

The bravest version of yourself

Dear Fellow Traveller,

As the letter I once wrote to myself reminds me, "This path we walk is paved with our own strength, even when it stretches into the unknown." When we face life's toughest challenges, it's easy to feel lost or overwhelmed. Yet every step forward, no matter how small, is a testament to your courage. Each moment of progress - however subtle - is a building block of resilience, a step closer to the peace and fulfilment you deserve.

Addiction often thrives in the shadows of isolation, feeding on disconnection from ourselves, others, and the world around us. Renowned author Johann Hari famously said, "The opposite of addiction is not sobriety. The opposite of addiction is connection." This profound insight speaks to the heart of recovery - our need for authentic, meaningful relationships and a sense of belonging.

Connection has the power to mend the fractures that addiction creates. It allows us to feel seen, heard, and understood, breaking the chains of loneliness and despair. Whether through the warmth of a shared smile, the safety of a supportive group, or the quiet strength of a trusted friend, connection weaves us back into the fabric of life. It reminds us that we are not alone and that healing is possible when we lean into others and open ourselves to vulnerability.

Yet, true connection begins within. It requires reconnection with your own heart and soul. It acknowledges your pain and honours your strength. As you rebuild this bond with yourself, you can extend it outward, creating a web of relationships that nurture and sustain you.

We all encounter pain, but it does not define us. Like the lotus that blooms from the mud, your struggles are not the end of your story – they are the fertile ground for your growth. Beneath the surface, your strength and beauty are waiting to emerge, even when circumstances feel heavy.

It's natural to have moments of doubt. When those whispers of disbelief creep in, remind yourself of the victories you've already claimed – big and small. Reflect on how far you've come and the incredible resilience you've shown. Even in the darkest moments, there is a flame within you, a light that refuses to be extinguished. Let it guide you through uncertainty and into a space of healing.

This journey is uniquely yours, and that is something to celebrate. Find peace in your quiet moments of growth, honour your progress, and remember that you are worthy – worthy of love, healing, and joy.

Connection – both to yourself and to others – can be your guiding light. It is the antidote to the isolation of addiction and the foundation of lasting recovery. Let it anchor you, nurture you, and remind you of the boundless potential within.

I believe in you deeply, just as the strongest and most hopeful version of yourself does. Hold onto that belief.

With all my love and unwavering support,

Warmly,

Vincenzia

CHAPTER 4 SUMMARY: THE HEALING POWER OF CONNECTION

FINDING SOLACE IN CONNECTION

Maya, a woman battling addiction, finds comfort in a group of strangers who provide a safe space for sharing pain and hope.

Through their stories, Maya realises she is part of a larger narrative of resilience and redemption, replacing her isolation with connection.

THE POWER OF STORIES

- Listening to others' stories of vulnerability and strength shifts Maya's perspective.
- Her story becomes a vital thread in the tapestry of collective hope and recovery.

THE SEASONS OF TRANSFORMATION

- Connection fuels Maya's recovery, offering stability amidst life's unpredictability.
- The support of her community mirrors the changing seasons, guiding her growth.

THE ANTIDOTE TO ADDICTION

- Maya discovers that healing comes through connection, not isolation.
- Her group dismantles addiction's illusion of isolation, showing how acceptance and understanding foster recovery.

THE FOUR PILLARS OF HEALING

- Maya's recovery is grounded in four pillars: belonging, joy, freedom, and love.
- These pillars empower her to navigate past challenges and embrace a hopeful future.

A SACRED SPACE FOR WHOLENESS

Maya's journey highlights how connection transforms pain into purpose.

The group becomes a sacred space, nurturing her transition from isolation to belonging.

THE FOUR PILLARS OF RECOVERY: A FRAMEWORK FOR WHOLENESS

1. Belonging: The Anchor of Connection

As a fundamental human need, belonging creates self-connection, community, and engagement with the world.

2. Joy: Cultivating Inner Light

Joy provides strength in recovery through meaningful attachments, savouring life, and personal growth.

3. Freedom: Breaking Free

Freedom involves reclaiming authenticity, breaking unhealthy patterns, and living with integrity.

4. Love: The Heart of Transformation

Love connects self-compassion, relationships, and giving to others, binding recovery into a cohesive journey.

PRACTICAL TOOLS FOR BUILDING THE FOUR PILLARS

- **Belonging**: Join recovery groups, seek therapy, or build a supportive network.
- **Joy**: Practice gratitude, engage in hobbies, and meditate.
- **Freedom**: Develop mindfulness, set boundaries, and challenge negative thought patterns.
- **Love**: Encourages self-compassion through affirmations and self-care routines.

THE TRANSFORMATIVE POWER OF CONNECTION

- Connection is essential for recovery, offering a sense of belonging, purpose, and emotional support.
- Strategies like social interaction, music therapy, outdoor activities, and vocational training rebuild meaningful connections.
- Recovery thrives not in isolation but in rediscovered purpose and engagement with others.

EMBRACING THE MUD: BECOMING THE LOTUS

- Like the lotus emerging from the mud, Maya learns to embrace challenges as opportunities for growth.
- Through mindfulness and introspection, adversity becomes the foundation for personal transformation and enlightenment.

THE DOMINO EFFECT: TRAUMA, RECOVERY, AND GROWTH

- Trauma and addiction are deeply intertwined, but recovery provides a unique chance for transformation.
- Maya's journey reflects how addressing trauma creates space for healing and personal growth.

REBUILDING WHOLENESS: THE CORE ELEMENTS OF RECOVERY

- Reconnect with Your Authentic Self: Rediscover who you are beyond addiction.
- Prioritise Physical Health: Adopt healthy lifestyle habits.
- Shift Negative Thinking: Cultivate positivity and self-compassion.
- Regulate Emotions: Acknowledge and process emotions healthily.
- Build Connections: Forge meaningful relationships.
- Find Meaning and Purpose: Align your life with values and aspirations.

UNDERSTANDING COGNITIVE DISTORTIONS IN RECOVERY

Negative thought patterns (e.g., all-or-nothing thinking, mental filtering) amplify disconnection and hinder recovery. CBT and DBT help challenge and reframe these distortions, fostering healthier perspectives.

SOBRIETY VS. RECOVERY

- **Sobriety**: Abstinence from addictive substances or behaviours.
- **Recovery**: A deeper journey addressing root causes, building skills, and fostering personal growth.

THE TRANSFORMATIVE POWER OF RECOVERY

Recovery is a profound process of renewal and self-discovery, marked by:

- **Reclaiming Your Authentic Self:** Embracing who you are without addiction.
- **Finding Purpose:** Exploring values and meaningful activities.
- **Healing Trauma:** Creating space for safety and processing past pain.
- **Fostering Connection:** Rebuilding trust and relationships.
- **Living a Balanced Life:** Promoting self-care and holistic well-being.
- **Giving Back:** Supporting others on their recovery journeys.

REFLECTION PROMPTS

Embracing the Mud: A Journey to the Lotus

- Have you ever faced a personal challenge or period of "mud" in your life? How did you manage it?
- Can you identify how your struggles have helped you grow and become a stronger person?
- Imagine yourself as the lotus seed submerged in the mud. What metaphorical "nourishment" do you draw from the challenges you face?
- Think of a time when you observed someone else overcome adversity. What qualities or actions did they possess that facilitated their growth?
- Consider a current challenge in your life. How can you "tend to the muck with care" and approach it in a way that promotes your growth?
- What practices or activities help you find peace and "tranquillity" amidst the chaos of life?

- Think of a time when you felt "unfurling" and experienced a sense of personal growth after overcoming a difficulty. Describe that experience.
- How can you incorporate the metaphor of the lotus flower into your daily life as a reminder of your own potential for transformation?
- Do you know anyone who has overcome addiction or a personal struggle? How can you support them on their journey?
- In your opinion, how can we create a more compassionate and supportive environment for individuals facing personal challenges, allowing them to "bloom" and reach their full potential?

RESOURCES

BOOKS

- ***The Gifts of Imperfection*** by Brené Brown: Explores vulnerability, courage, and authenticity.
- ***Lost Connections*** by Johann Harie examines societal factors contributing to depression and proposes solutions.
- ***The Power of Now*** by Eckhart Tolle focuses on living in the present moment and finding inner peace.
- ***Daring Greatly*** by Brené Brown delves into vulnerability and its role in fostering authentic connections.
- ***The Unexpected Joy of Being Sober*** by Catherine Gray shares a personal journey of recovery and finding joy in sobriety.
- ***The Body Keeps the Score*** by Bessel van der Kolk explores the effects of trauma on the body and mind and offers healing strategies.

YOUTUBE

- Brené Brown's TED Talks: Discusses vulnerability, shame, and connection.
- Johann Hari's Talks: Explores societal factors contributing to depression and recommends solutions.
- Eckhart Tolle's Teachings: Focuses on mindfulness, presence, and inner peace.
- Recovery Stories: Personal stories of addiction recovery and finding healing.
- Mental Health Channels: Offers insights on coping strategies, self-care, and resilience.
- Guided Meditations: Provides tools for personal growth and transformation.
- Authenticity and Addiction Recovery: Discusses the role of authenticity in recovery.
- Understanding Trauma: Explores the connection between trauma and mental health.

PODCASTS

- ***Unlocking Us*** with Brené Brown explores vulnerability, courage, shame, and empathy.
- ***The Mental Illness Happy Hour*** features candid conversations about mental health, addiction, and trauma.
- ***The Recovery Show*** focuses on addiction recovery and 12-step programs.
- ***The One You Feed*** explores personal growth, resilience, and well-being.

- ***The Trauma Therapist Podcast*** explores trauma and recovery.
- ***Meditative Story*** combines storytelling with meditation.
- ***The Tim Ferriss Show*** features interviews with guests who share strategies for overcoming challenges and finding fulfilment.

CHAPTER 5 - RECLAIMING WHOLENESS

A MOSAIC OF HEALING: FROM SHATTERED PIECES TO A LUMINOUS MASTERPIECE

In the quiet corner of a grand cathedral, a dusty box overflows with fractured memories. Each shard of glass, once a luminous piece of an impressive stained-glass window, bears the scars of a life upended. Spider web cracks trace the contours of struggles endured, and jagged edges speak of impacts weathered. Yet, amidst the splintered remnants, glimmers of forgotten brilliance remain – a reminder of the beauty that once was and can be again.

An old maestro, famed for crafting breathtaking stained-glass windows, kneels before the box. Where others see brokenness, he sees potential. His hands move with reverence, lifting each shard up to the light and envisioning its place in a new creation.

Like the maestro, you, too, can find potential within the fractured pieces of yourself. Each shard represents a moment of struggle: a severed connection, a hidden emotion, or a shattered dream. Recovery is the artful process of holding these pieces up, acknowledging their weight, and discovering their inherent strength. It's a meticulous yet soul-stirring task, crafting your life into a breathtaking mosaic of healing.

When the masterpiece is complete – each shard thoughtfully placed, each fracture transformed into part of a grand design – it is gently set into the cathedral wall. As sunlight streams through, the window bursts to life in a kaleidoscope of colours. The once-dim cathedral is instantly transformed, bathed in a cascade of radiant hues. Shadows dissolve, and the interplay of light and colour breathes new energy into the sacred space.

In the same way, reclaiming your wholeness can transform your life. Each piece of your journey – no matter how broken or painful – is an integral part of the brilliant masterpiece you are becoming. With patience and self-compassion, the fragments of your past can coalesce into something profoundly beautiful, illuminating not only your life but also the lives of those around you.

This is the power of compassionate recovery: to turn shattered pieces into a source of light, hope, and transformation. Through this mosaic of healing, you rediscover not only yourself but also your place in the larger tapestry of life. Like the stained-glass window, your unique brilliance shines most beautifully when illuminated by love, resilience, and the warmth of connection.

THE ROAD TO WHOLENESS

Addiction is like a relentless tide, eroding the foundation of your being. It fragments the ties that bind your mind, body, and soul, severing your connection to community, nature, and your authentic self. In its wake, it leaves a profound yearning, a deep hunger to rediscover your true essence and witness it bloom. Yet, this longing is often drowned by the noise of numbing behaviours and the endless pursuit of fleeting relief.

Beneath the surface, however, there is a persistent whisper – a quiet, steadfast call to follow a different path. It is the voice of your true self urging you to embark on a wayfinding quest of reconnection. This chapter serves as your navigational instrument, guiding you toward wholeness – a journey of profound integration and healing.

Reclaiming wholeness is about charting a new course through the uncharted waters of recovery. It is a wayfinding quest, an exploration of reconnecting the parts of yourself that have been scattered, misaligned, or forgotten.

THE WAYFINDING QUEST OF RECONNECTION

- **Reconnecting with Yourself**: Embrace your authentic identity, honouring both your imperfections and strengths. Delve deep to heal past traumas and rediscover the dreams that once inspired you. See yourself not as broken but as whole, with infinite potential to grow and thrive.
- **Reconnecting with Others**: Build relationships that uplift, encourage, and remind you of the power of belonging. Connection is a lifeline, a compass that reorients you toward love, acceptance, and understanding.
- **Reconnecting with the Natural World**: The rhythms of nature mirror the cycles of life and recovery. Allow the natural world to ground you, its beauty and constancy offering healing and a sense of perspective as you navigate your way forward.
- **Reconnecting with Purpose**: Align your actions with your deepest values, rediscovering the sense of meaning that propels you toward fulfilment. Purpose is the north star that guides your journey through the unknown.

- **Reconnecting Spiritually**: Whether through faith, mindfulness, or awe for life's mysteries, cultivate a spiritual connection that provides clarity, peace, and unity with something greater than yourself.

Healing is a dynamic process of rediscovery and integration. This wayfinding quest is about becoming who you are meant to be. With each step, you reclaim the fragments of your being, placing them into a luminous mosaic of resilience, love, and strength.

Trust the process, and trust yourself. Every step, no matter how small, brings you closer to the vibrant wholeness that has always been your birthright. This is your journey, your navigation toward the fullest, most authentic version of yourself. Embrace it with courage.

THE PATH TO RECONNECTION: LETTING GO AND MOVING FORWARD

Reconnecting with your true self, others, and the world is a profound journey. This journey requires not only seeking but also releasing. Much like crossing monkey bars, progress in life demands letting go of what no longer serves you to grasp what lies ahead. Each bar you hold represents a belief, habit, relationship, or coping mechanism. To move forward, you must release one bar before reaching for the next. Reconnection and growth follow the same principle: letting go of what holds you back creates space for meaningful transformation.

RECONNECTING THROUGH LETTING GO

True reconnection is not about adding new experiences but creating space for them by releasing what no longer aligns with your values and aspirations. Whether it's a toxic relationship, an outdated self-perception, or an unhealthy coping mechanism, letting go clears the path for authentic connection and growth.

- **Letting Go of Old Identities:** Addiction and trauma often bind us to identities rooted in shame or self-doubt. Releasing allows you to embrace the person you are becoming.
- **Shedding Harmful Relationships:** Some connections tether you to the past, reinforcing pain or dysfunction. Releasing these connections allows healthier bonds to form.
- **Releasing Limiting Beliefs:** False narratives like "I am unworthy" can stifle growth. Letting go of these beliefs encourages self-compassion and empowerment.

LESSONS FROM LETTING GO

- **Creates Space for Growth:** Releasing what no longer serves you opens new opportunities and perspectives.
- **Momentum Builds Confidence:** Each act of letting go reinforces your ability to progress.
- **Growth Is Incremental:** True transformation happens one step at a time, with each small action propelling you forward.

HEALING THE FRACTURED SELF: PAVING THE WAY TO WHOLENESS

Addiction fragments life, straining relationships, compromising health, and leaving the self divided. Recovery is a process of reintegration – mending relationships, nurturing emotional well-being, and healing traumas. Achieving wholeness requires both reclaiming and releasing. Just as an artist discards broken tools to create a masterpiece, healing asks that you release the fragments of your past to make room for authenticity and growth.

- **Introspection:** Begin by revisiting the roots of disconnection. What unmet needs, traumas, or beliefs have shaped your coping mechanisms?
- **Identifying Needs:** Reflect on areas where you feel lacking – such as safety, belonging, or recognition – and explore how these unmet needs manifest in your life.

MEETING YOUR NEEDS IN HEALTHY WAYS

Once you've identified your needs, adopt strategies to address them sustainably:

- **Self-Care Practices:** Regular exercise, nourishing meals, mindfulness, and journaling.
- **Support Networks:** Therapy, support groups, or relationships that nurture growth.
- **Creative Outlets:** Pursue hobbies and activities that inspire joy and passion.
- **Nature Connection:** Spend time outdoors to ground yourself and find solace.
- **Continuous Growth:** Explore new learning opportunities and challenges that spark curiosity.

RECLAIMING WHOLENESS: A DANCE OF INTEGRATION AND RELEASE

Healing is a dynamic balance between holding on to what heals and letting go of what harms. Each release – whether it's an outdated belief, toxic attachment, or harmful habit – creates space for growth. Letting go is an act of courage and trust, allowing you to reach for the next phase of your journey.

Recovery is about embracing every piece of yourself – both fractured and whole – and weaving them together with self-compassion. Each step forward transforms the mosaic of your life into a masterpiece of resilience, authenticity, and beauty.

CHANGE AND WHOLENESS THROUGH THE LENS OF NEUROPLASTICITY

The human brain is a marvel of adaptability, capable of incredible change and growth through neuroplasticity. This inherent flexibility allows the brain to rewire itself, creating, strengthening, and reorganising neural pathways to form new patterns of thought, emotion, and behaviour. Neuroplasticity forms the foundation for learning, memory, and recovery, offering the opportunity to break free from negative cycles and cultivating integration, healing, and wholeness.

More than a scientific concept, neuroplasticity offers hope. It highlights the brain's ability to heal from trauma and overcome entrenched patterns of behaviour and thought. Trauma imprints itself on neural networks, shaping how we perceive and respond to the world. Yet, these patterns are not permanent, and change is possible.

THE ROLE OF NEUROPLASTICITY IN HEALING

Neuroplasticity enables individuals to:

- **Rewire the Brain:** Healthy experiences and habits create new neural connections, weakening those linked to trauma or harmful behaviours.

- **Strengthen Resilience:** Positive coping mechanisms, emotional regulation, and adaptability foster resilience.
- **Break Cycles of Generational Trauma:** Addressing inherited patterns of trauma paves the way for healthier relationships and well-being for future generations.

EMPOWERING CHANGE THROUGH NEUROPLASTICITY

Transformation thrives on deliberate effort. By understanding neuroplasticity, you can intentionally reshape your neural pathways through:

- **Learning and Growth:** Engage in activities that challenge the brain, such as learning new skills or creative pursuits.
- **Mindfulness and Meditation:** Practices like meditation reduce stress, improve focus, and support emotional regulation.
- **Healthy Habits:** Regular physical activity, balanced nutrition, and adequate sleep enhance brain health.
- **Therapeutic Interventions:** Trauma-informed therapies such as EMDR, somatic experiencing, or CBT harness neuroplasticity to heal trauma.
- **Support Networks:** Strong relationships create safety and belonging, essential for healing and growth.

DISRUPTING GENERATIONAL TRAUMA

Through intentional healing, you can disrupt cycles of intergenerational trauma. By rewiring the brain through therapy, education, and trauma-informed approaches, healing extends beyond the individual, positively influencing family dynamics and benefiting future generations.

CHARACTERISTICS OF NEUROPLASTICITY

- **Adaptability:** Like a muscle, the brain grows stronger with regular use, supporting growth and flexibility.
- **Dynamic Connections:** Neural pathways are strengthened or weakened based on experiences and actions.
- **Lifelong Learning:** The brain retains its malleability throughout life, enabling continuous growth.
- **Recovery and Healing:** Neuroplasticity allows the brain to self-repair, creating new pathways to overcome adversity.

APPLICATIONS IN MENTAL HEALTH

- **Addiction Recovery:** CBT and mindfulness weaken addiction-related pathways, promoting healthier coping mechanisms.
- **Trauma Resilience:** Therapies like EMDR and somatic experiencing release trauma and restore balance.
- **Cognitive Restructuring:** Approaches like CBT, ACT, and DBT promote healthier thought patterns and emotional regulation.
- **Stress Reduction:** Mindfulness-based stress reduction (MBSR) enhances well-being by leveraging neuroplasticity.
- **Creative Therapies:** Art and music therapy engage neural networks, encouraging healing and exploration.

RECLAIMING WHOLENESS THROUGH NEUROPLASTICITY

Wholeness requires letting go. Just as the brain weakens old neural pathways to forge new ones, recovery involves releasing harmful patterns, beliefs, and attachments. Healing is not about "fixing" but about reintegrating fragmented parts into a cohesive, empowered whole.

- **Letting Go of Old Patterns**: Relinquishing outdated behaviours and relationships creates space for growth.
- **Building New Pathways**: Therapy, mindfulness, and creative pursuits strengthen healthier networks.

HEALING AS A COLLECTIVE JOURNEY

Neuroplasticity emphasises the interconnectedness of personal, societal, and environmental well-being. Individual healing contributes to stronger, more compassionate communities, creating a ripple effect of resilience and empathy.

INTEGRATION AND GROWTH

Healing through neuroplasticity is a journey of integration. Past wounds become stepping stones to resilience, allowing you to reclaim your wholeness. By shaping healthier neural pathways, you encourage a future of connection and harmony.

Embracing the brain's potential to heal and grow empowers you to rewrite your narrative and create a meaningful life. This transformative journey not only reclaims personal wholeness but also contributes to a more compassionate world.

Dear Fellow Traveller,

As you embark on the incredible journey toward reclaiming wholeness, I extend to you a heartfelt embrace and deep recognition of the courage it takes to choose this path. Know that this journey is not only personal but intricately woven into the broader tapestry of life – a fabric where individual healing strengthens the resilience of our communities and the vitality of our planet.

Addiction casts its shadow not only over our inner lives but also across the ecosystems we inhabit, the communities we cherish, and the generations yet to come. Its echoes challenge us to face the harsh realities of disconnection with courage and a determination to restore balance. Yet within these challenges lies a profound truth: to move forward, we must first let go.

Letting go is an act of grace. Like a traveller, we must lift our feet to move forward; we cannot step into growth without first releasing the foot behind us. Letting go of pain, old habits, limiting beliefs, and the false safety of addiction clears the path for reconnection – with ourselves, with others, and with the world. This act of release creates space for the light of transformation to enter, illuminating the potential that lies ahead.

Within each of us resides a boundless reservoir of transformative power fuelled by love, compassion, and interconnectedness. This power calls us to rise above the grips of addiction and embrace the complexities of our existence with resilience and grace. It is through this sacred work that we lay the foundation for a society that prioritises the well-being of all beings and the preservation of our shared Earth.

True healing reaches beyond the self. It touches our relationships, strengthens our communities, and nurtures the natural world. Together, we commit to a collective journey of profound transformation – a journey that transcends the confines of addiction and propels us toward a future guided by harmony, compassion, and sustainable living.

As you journey onward, remember this: the strength to heal lies within you, waiting to be rediscovered. With every act of letting go, you make space for renewal, growth, and connection. Through empathy, love, and compassion, we co-create a world where all beings thrive in unity and interconnectedness.

With warm regards and boundless solidarity,

Vincenzia

CHAPTER 5 SUMMARY

THE MOSAIC OF HEALING: FROM SHATTERED PIECES TO A LUMINOUS MASTERPIECE

- The story is about a stained-glass window with fragmented memories, each representing a moment of struggle.
- Recovery is the process of acknowledging these fragments and discovering their inherent strength.
- The mosaic of healing is a reflection of the transformation of one's life.
- The fragments of the past can coalesce into something profoundly beautiful, illuminating not only one's life but also those around it.

THE ROAD TO WHOLENESS

- Addiction is like a relentless tide, eroding the foundation of one's being.
- It leaves a deep yearning to rediscover one's true essence and witness it bloom.
- The voice of the true self, buried yet unbroken, urging one to embark on a wayfinding quest of reconnection.
- Reclaiming wholeness is not just about mending what was broken but about charting a new course through the uncharted waters of recovery.

THE WAYFINDING QUEST OF RECONNECTION

- **Reconnecting with Yourself:** Embrace your authentic identity, honouring both your imperfections and strengths.
- **Reconnecting with Others:** Build relationships that uplift, encourage, and remind you of the power of belonging.
- **Reconnecting with the Natural World:** Allow the natural world to ground you, offering healing and a sense of perspective.

- **Reconnecting with Purpose:** Align your actions with your deepest values, rediscovering the sense of meaning that propels you toward fulfilment.
- **Reconnecting Spiritually:** Cultivate a spiritual connection that provides clarity, peace, and unity with something greater than yourself.

Healing is not a linear path – it is a dynamic process of rediscovery and integration.

THE PATH TO RECONNECTION: LETTING GO AND MOVING FORWARD

Reconnecting Through Letting Go

Reconnecting with oneself, others, and the world requires releasing what no longer serves, whether it is limiting beliefs, emotional burdens, or patterns that keep us stuck in the past. Often, we hold onto these attachments out of fear, familiarity, or a mistaken sense of identity, even when they hinder our ability to grow. True connection can only flourish when we create space for it, and that begins with letting go of what weighs us down. By shedding toxic relationships, outdated self-perceptions, and unhealthy coping mechanisms, we make room for deeper self-awareness, meaningful relationships, and a more fulfilling life. The act of releasing is about opening ourselves to something greater: authenticity, freedom, and the ability to engage with life wholeheartedly.

Lessons from Letting Go

- It creates space for growth, builds confidence, and promotes incremental growth.
- It also opens new opportunities and perspectives.

HEALING THE FRACTURED SELF: PAVING THE WAY TO WHOLENESS

- Recovery involves reintegration, repairing relationships, nurturing emotional well-being, and healing traumas.
- Healing involves releasing past fragments to make room for authenticity and growth. Strategies for embracing one's unique and authentic self may include prioritising self-care, cultivating supportive relationships, exploring creative outlets, setting aside time to connect with nature, and engaging in activities that foster personal growth and well-being.

RECLAIMING WHOLENESS: A DANCE OF INTEGRATION AND RELEASE

- Healing involves finding a balance between holding on to what heals and letting go of what harms.
- Each release creates space for growth.
- Recovery is about embracing every piece of oneself and weaving them together with self-compassion.

CHANGE AND WHOLENESS THROUGH THE LENS OF NEUROPLASTICITY

- Neuroplasticity allows the brain to rewire itself, forming new patterns of thought, emotion, and behaviour.
- It offers hope and highlights the brain's ability to heal from trauma and overcome entrenched patterns of behaviour and thought.

NEUROPLASTICITY IN HEALING AND ITS APPLICATIONS

Role of Neuroplasticity in Healing

- Neuroplasticity allows us to rewire our brains, strengthen resilience, and break cycles of intergenerational trauma.

- Transformation thrives on deliberate effort and can be achieved through learning and growth, mindfulness and meditation, healthy habits, therapeutic interventions, and strong relationships.

Disrupting Generational Trauma

Through intentional healing, we can disrupt cycles of intergenerational trauma, positively influencing family dynamics and benefiting future generations.

Characteristics of Neuroplasticity

- **Adaptability:** The brain grows stronger with regular use, supporting growth and flexibility.
- **Dynamic Connections:** Neural pathways are strengthened or weakened based on experiences and actions.
- **Lifelong Learning:** The brain retains its malleability throughout life, enabling continuous growth.
- **Recovery and Healing:** Neuroplasticity allows the brain to self-repair, creating new pathways to overcome adversity.

Applications in Mental Health

- **Addiction Recovery:** Cognitive Behavioural Therapy (CBT) and mindfulness weaken addiction-related pathways, fostering healthier coping mechanisms.
- **Trauma Resilience:** Therapies like EMDR and somatic experiencing release trauma and restore balance.
- **Cognitive Restructuring:** Approaches like CBT, ACT, and DBT promote healthier thought patterns and emotional regulation.
- **Stress Reduction:** Mindfulness-based stress reduction (MBSR) enhances well-being by leveraging neuroplasticity.

- **Creative Therapies:** Art and music therapy engage neural networks, fostering healing and exploration.

Reclaiming Wholeness Through Neuroplasticity

- Healing involves releasing harmful patterns, beliefs, and attachments and reintegrating fragmented parts into a cohesive whole.
- **Building New Pathways:** Therapy, mindfulness, and creative pursuits strengthen healthier networks.
- **Healing as a Collective Journey:** Neuroplasticity emphasises the interconnectedness of personal, societal, and environmental well-being.
- **Integration and Growth:** Healing through neuroplasticity is a journey of integration, allowing individuals to reclaim their wholeness.

RESOURCES

BOOKS

Discover valuable insights on addiction, trauma, neuroplasticity, and healing:

- ***The Biology of Desire: Why Addiction Is Not a Disease*** by Marc Lewis explores recovery and underlying causes.
- ***The Body Keeps the Score: Brain, Mind, and Body in the Healing of Trauma*** by Bessel van der Kolk offers a guide to healing the fractured self.
- ***The Body Remembers: The Psychophysiology of Trauma and Trauma Treatment*** by Babette Rothschild delves into fractured societies and historical trauma.
- ***It Didn't Start with You: How Inherited Family Trauma Shapes Who We Are*** by Mark Wolynn examines epigenetics and generational trauma.

- ***The Brain That Changes Itself: Stories of Personal Triumph*** by Norman Doidge highlights neuroplasticity's transformative power.
- ***Train Your Mind, Change Your Brain*** by Sharon Begley discusses neuroplasticity's role in mental health and therapy.
- ***Lost Connections: Uncovering the Real Causes of Depression*** by Johann Hari reimagines addiction and power with a focus on compassion and environmental consciousness.
- ***The Soul of an Octopus*** by Sy Montgomery explores reclaiming wholeness through consciousness and connection.

YOUTUBE CHANNELS

Explore expert discussions on addiction, trauma, and healing:

- **Bessel van der Kolk:** Led by Dr Bessel van der Kolk: This channel delves into trauma, healing, and mental health.
- **Psychology in Seattle:** Hosted by Dr Kirk Honda: Addresses addiction, trauma, and therapeutic approaches.
- **Rewire Your Brain for Love:** Marci J. Shimoff: Explores neuroplasticity, mindfulness, and personal growth for love and well-being.

SECTION 2: DIRECT GUIDANCE FOR YOUR RECOVERY

Welcome to the second part of this book, a collection of self-contained chapters created to speak directly to you. In this section, each chapter stands alone as a practical resource, complete with its own explanation of CR, ensuring that you have all the necessary insights and tools at your fingertips. Whether you're reading independently or working with a coach, therapist, or counsellor, you can focus on the chapter that addresses your current needs without feeling compelled to work through the entire book.

This structure has been designed with your journey in mind. By offering targeted, standalone content, the material becomes more accessible and flexible, allowing you to tackle specific issues as they arise. Each chapter is an invitation to explore a distinct aspect of recovery, giving you the freedom to choose the guidance that resonates most with your personal experience.

For coaches, therapists, or counsellors, this structure allows you to assign a single chapter to a client in recovery, allowing them to focus on specific issues without needing to navigate the entire book.

Embrace this section as your individualised roadmap, a collection of insights and strategies meant to support you wherever you are in your recovery process.

CHAPTER 6 - EXPLORING FRAMEWORKS FOR COMPASSIONATE RECOVERY

Recovery is a deeply personal journey, and no single path suits everyone. This section introduces three distinct frameworks – **Martha Beck's Change Cycle**, the original **Four Cardinal Directions**, and the **8 C's of Self-Leadership** – designed to guide transformation. Complementing these, I have created a companion book, *The 12 Stepping Stones: A Practical Path to Healing and Wholeness*. This book provides 12 actionable steps for navigating recovery.

I created *The 12 Stepping Stones* to work in tandem with this book. While From Pain to Purpose lays the foundation for understanding the journey of recovery, this guide offers a practical, step-by-step pathway toward healing and wholeness. Each of the stepping stones has been personally designed to support you as you navigate your recovery process, and each one explores a unique mindfulness practice or attitude. This approach provides clear, hands-on strategies and exercises that empower you to apply the principles discussed in the main book to real-life situations, facilitating both personal growth and sustained healing.

THE ADAPTATION OF MARTHA BECK'S CHANGE CYCLE

Martha Beck's **Change Cycle**, adapted for **Compassionate Recovery (CR)**, provides a structured approach to transformation with four distinct phases:

- **Death and Rebirth:** Confront the loss of old patterns, sitting with discomfort to foster self-compassion.
- **Dreaming and Scheming:** Explore new hobbies, possibilities, and resilience, balancing creativity with patience.
- **The Hero's Saga:** Test new behaviours, manage setbacks, and build healthy routines with perseverance and community support.
- **The Promised Land:** Embrace integration by applying learned skills, cultivating gratitude, and giving back, ensuring sustained growth and balance.

This framework simplifies the complexities associated with recovery, offering actionable strategies for each stage. Its cyclical nature normalises setbacks as part of growth, empowering you to rebuild your life with clarity, compassion, and resilience.

THE 8 CS OF SELF-LEADERSHIP

The 8 Cs of Self-Leadership are:

1. Curiosity
2. Courage
3. Clarity
4. Compassion
5. Creativity
6. Confidence
7. Connectedness
8. Calmness

These are foundational to CR and promote balance and fulfilment.

Core Benefits

- **Resilience:** Build the strength to navigate setbacks with emotional fortitude.
- **Self-Awareness:** Understand behaviours deeply and address root causes.
- **Emotional Regulation:** Manage emotions constructively, reducing impulsivity.
- **Healthy Relationships:** Strengthen interpersonal dynamics and connection.
- **Sustainable Growth:** Extend recovery beyond abstinence to thriving personal growth.

THE 4 CARDINAL DIRECTIONS: A COMPASS FOR RECOVERY

The Four Cardinal Directions are:

1. Responsibility
2. Acceptance
3. Forgiveness
4. Hope

These directions serve as guiding principles for overcoming life's challenges and align with CR's values of empowerment and transformation.

Core Principles

- **Responsibility:** Focus on intentional responses to challenges, creating self-awareness and agency.
- **Acceptance:** Embrace reality without resistance, creating space for healing and growth.
- **Forgiveness:** Release resentment and shame, opening pathways to freedom and self-compassion.
- **Hope:** Nurture optimism and motivation to strengthen resilience, even in the face of uncertainty. This framework provides a practical and empowering roadmap for recovery, helping you navigate challenges with clarity and courage.

THE 12 STEPPING STONES: A PRACTICAL PATH TO HEALING AND WHOLENESS

A Companion Book

The 12 Stepping Stones is a practical guide that bridges abstract ideals with real-world application, offering structured steps for emotional recovery, self-discovery, and personal growth.

Purpose and Focus

- To address challenges with addiction, trauma, and personal transformation.
- To introduce mindfulness practices and techniques.
- To support alignment with core values and a holistic mindfulness-based approach to healing.

How It Supports Your Journey

Like stepping stones across uncertain terrain, each principle offers a stable foundation to help you move from pain to balance and fulfilment. Paired with CR frameworks, this guide provides a structured and compassionate approach to recovery.

HOW TO CHOOSE THE FRAMEWORK THAT SUITS YOUR CURRENT NEEDS

Selecting the most suitable framework for your recovery journey depends on your current challenges, emotional readiness, and personal goals. Here's a guide to help you decide:

1. Assess Your Current Challenges

Start by reflecting on what feels most pressing or overwhelming in your life.

1. Are you struggling with uncertainty or feeling stuck?

   Framework: *Martha Beck's Change Cycle* helps you understand where you are in the transformation process and provides clarity for your next steps.

2. Do you feel disconnected from yourself or others?

   Framework: *The 4 Cardinal Directions* emphasise principles like responsibility, forgiveness, and hope to restore connection and purpose.

3. Are you seeking emotional stability and personal growth?

   Framework: *The 8 Cs of Self-Leadership* focuses on cultivating inner qualities like courage, calmness, and clarity to help you build resilience.

4. Do you need actionable steps for navigating recovery?

   Framework: *The 12 Stepping Stones* provides practical guidance for bridging the gap between abstract ideals and real-world change.

2. Consider Your Readiness for Inner Work

- If you're just beginning and feel overwhelmed, start with frameworks that focus on stability and clarity, like The *Change Cycle* or *Four Cardinal Directions*.
- If you feel ready for deeper emotional exploration, *The 8 Cs of Self-Leadership* provide tools for self-awareness and addressing root causes.

- If you prefer structured, step-by-step guidance, *The 12 Stepping Stones Companion Guide* offers a clear and actionable roadmap.

3. Align with Your Goals

Match the framework to the outcomes you're seeking.

- **Clarity and direction:** Martha Beck's *Change Cycle* helps map the journey and anticipate challenges.
- **Emotional healing and connection:** *The Four Cardinal Directions* promotes self-compassion and interpersonal growth.
- **Personal growth and balance:** *The 8 Cs of Self-Leadership* supports building inner resilience and thriving.
- **Practical transformation:** *The 12 Stepping Stones* bridges ideals and actionable change.

4. Identify Your Preferred Approach

Think about how you like to process challenges:

- **Big-picture thinkers:** *The Change Cycle* offers a phased approach to understanding transformation.
- **Values-driven individuals:** *Four Cardinal Directions* focuses on principles like acceptance and hope.
- **Quality-focused explorers:** *8 Cs* emphasises cultivating internal strengths.
- **Action-oriented doers:** *12 Stepping Stones* provides step-by-step tasks for progression.

5. Experiment and Adapt

- Since your needs may evolve, you don't have to commit to just one framework.
- Start with the framework that feels most immediately relevant.
- Reflect regularly on whether it's meeting your needs.
- Mix and match elements from different frameworks as your journey progresses.

6. Seek Guidance

If you're uncertain, consider consulting a coach, therapist, or trusted guide who can help you evaluate your situation and recommend a starting point.

7. Trust Your Intuition

You know yourself best. Trust your instincts when deciding which framework resonates most with your current state.

Choosing the right framework is about aligning it with your current challenges, readiness, and goals. Recovery is a dynamic journey, and as you grow, your needs may shift. Start where you feel most comfortable and remain open to exploring additional frameworks as your understanding deepens and your resilience builds.

Dear Fellow Traveller,

As you embark on your recovery journey, I want to acknowledge your courage in taking these first steps. Recovery is not a one-size-fits-all path – it's a deeply personal and evolving process. Compassionate recovery is about finding what resonates with your heart, addressing your unique challenges, and honouring your readiness to grow and heal.

To support you, I've gathered a few frameworks that may serve as a compass on this journey. Each offers a different perspective, allowing you to choose the one that aligns best with your current needs.

If you feel overwhelmed or unsure of where to begin, Martha Beck's Change Cycle may provide clarity. Its four phases – Death and Rebirth, Dreaming and Scheming, The Hero's Saga, and The Promised Land – map out the transformation process, helping you navigate moments of discomfort and celebrate milestones of growth.

If your heart longs for guiding principles, The Four Cardinal Directions – Responsibility, Acceptance, Forgiveness, and Hope – offer timeless wisdom. These directions can ground you in self-awareness, acceptance, and optimism, helping you embrace life's challenges with grace and courage.

For those ready to dive inward, the 8 Cs of Self-Leadership – Curiosity, Courage, Clarity, Compassion, Creativity, Confidence, Connectedness, and Calmness – can help you cultivate the qualities needed to thrive. These are tools to navigate emotional turbulence, foster resilience, and deepen your connection to yourself and others.

If you prefer actionable steps, The 12 Stepping Stones: A Practical Path to Healing and Wholeness might be your guide. Like stepping stones across uncertain terrain, each principle - mindfulness, self-compassion, impermanence, and more - offers stability as you move toward a life of balance and fulfilment.

There is no "right" place to start - there is only the place that feels most meaningful to you. Recovery is a journey marked by progress, setbacks, and growth. Trust that each step, no matter how small, carries you closer to wholeness.

Remember, you don't have to walk this path alone. Surround yourself with supportive people, and don't hesitate to seek guidance when you need it. Each framework is a companion, a light to guide your way, but the most important compass is within you.

You are not defined by where you've been but by the courage you show as you move forward. May these tools and principles empower you to navigate your journey with clarity, compassion, and hope.

With warmth and solidarity,

Vincenzia,

A Fellow Traveller

CHAPTER 7 - THE JOURNEY INWARD: COMPASSIONATE RECOVERY AND THE POWER OF SELF-AWARENESS

ALL THAT GLITTERS IS NOT GOLD

In a bustling city, amidst the chaos of the busy streets, lived a young crow named Corvus. His dreams soared higher than the towering skyscrapers, yearning for a place amongst the graceful ravens that ruled the urban skies. One fateful day, a glint of gold caught Corvus's eye in a grimy alleyway: a shiny necklace, discarded yet radiant, promised a shortcut to glory. Fuelled by misplaced hope, Corvus seized the trinket, convinced it was his ticket to the esteemed world of the ravens. With the glittery treasure draped ostentatiously around his neck, Corvus strutted through the city park, basking in the admiring glances of pigeons and sparrows. Yet, beneath the façade of pride, a gnawing disquiet plagued him. The once playful companions, the squirrels, now darted away with suspicion in their eyes. His attempts at mimicking the ravens' deep caws echoed his growing sense of alienation. The weight of the necklace, more than mere metal, bore down on him as a burden of inauthenticity.

Exhausted from the charade, Corvus found solace on a quiet branch, where a sigh of relief escaped his beak. The necklace, heavy not just with metal but with the weight of pretence, felt cumbersome. In a moment of clarity, he realised that true power wasn't nestled in the fleeting thrill of stolen trinkets or the hollow satisfaction of material gain. It dawned on him that real strength came from something far deeper: refining his abilities through dedication, hard work, and relentless practice. Mastery was not a gift but a craft. His power lay in the unshakeable foundation of his authentic self, the courage to embrace his flaws, and the conviction to stand tall without needing to mask his weaknesses behind illusions. Power, he understood, was rooted in the courage to be entirely, unapologetically himself. With newfound resolve, he cast the necklace aside, embracing his identity as a crow. Strength and freedom, he vowed, would be achieved on his own terms.

In the days that followed, Corvus embarked on his journey with unwavering dedication. Each dawn found him perched atop the tallest spire, his keen eyes scanning the sprawling city below. With relentless determination, he honed his flying skills, pushing himself to new heights of agility and precision. The bustling city became his playground, its tangled streets and towering skyscrapers his training grounds. As weeks turned into months, Corvus's senses became finely tuned instruments, attuned to every nuance of the urban landscape. The cacophony of sounds, the kaleidoscope of colours, all melded into a harmony of information that he effortlessly deciphered. No detail escaped his keen gaze – no obstacle impeded his path. In the crucible of the city's chaos, Corvus emerged not just as a proficient flyer but as a true master of the skies. His wings beat with purpose, his movements a testament to the bond between bird and urban jungle. Though not a raven, Corvus became a formidable crow, respected for his resourcefulness and skills.

One stormy afternoon, when a thunderstorm raged with unrestrained fury, Corvus's newfound strength faced its ultimate trial. The city skyline was obscured by a veil of dark clouds, and the streets below churned with the tumult of wind and rain. In the centre of the chaos, a young raven, its wings buffeted by the gales, found itself lost and bewildered, its mournful cries echoing through the storm. In that moment, a deeper understanding bloomed within Corvus. He recognised not just his own strength but the interconnectedness of all living things. The storm raged on, indifferent to species or status. As a crow, he had a unique ability to manage the chaos. This was a responsibility assigned not just to himself but to any creature in need.

With a heart that beat with empathy born from his own journey of self-discovery, Corvus soared into action. His wings sliced through the driving rain as he searched tirelessly for the distressed fledgling. Finally, amidst the swirling turbulence, he spotted the young raven, its feathers sodden and its spirit nearly broken. Approaching the trembling bird with confidence, Corvus extended a reassuring wing. Through gentle gestures and comforting chirps, he guided the fledgling to safety, leading it to shelter beneath the protective eaves of a nearby building. As the storm raged on, the grateful gaze of the young raven spoke volumes, affirming a vital truth. It was not the adornments of feathers or the accolades of flight that defined one's worth, but rather the journey of authenticity, self-discovery, and connection to others. In that moment, amidst the chaos of the storm, Corvus comprehended that true strength lay not in the mastery of the skies alone but in the compassion and empathy that bound all creatures together in the fabric of life.

Corvus's journey reveals an important truth: "All that glitters is not gold." True value lies not in external trappings or fleeting accolades but in the quiet resilience of authentic self-discovery. His flight to greatness wasn't gilded by imitation or the allure of shortcuts – rather, it was forged through the relentless pursuit of inner strength and mastery. In the end, Corvus understood that real power is not defined by how high we soar alone but by our capacity to lift others along the way. Genuine well-being is found not in seeking validation from others but in promoting compassion, humility, and gratitude for our own path. In a world obsessed with appearances, Corvus's tale reminds us that the true measure of success lies in embracing our own identity and sharing our gifts with those around us.

THE POWER OF YOUR INNER WORLD

Modern society often equates happiness with external markers such as wealth, possessions, and social status. The evidence suggests otherwise. Social media magnifies this illusion, presenting carefully curated images of luxury and success. Research, including pioneering work by psychologist Ed Diener, uncovers that external factors contribute to only about 10% of our overall well-being. The other 90% is determined by our internal world, which consists of our thoughts, attitudes, and actions. This inner realm shapes our emotional experiences and holds the key to achieving lasting happiness and fulfilment.

- **Thoughts:** The way we speak to ourselves has an unmistakable impact on our emotional well-being. Negative thought patterns can lead to a downward spiral, whereas nurturing positive thinking promotes resilience and optimism.
- **Attitudes:** Our beliefs about ourselves and the world shape the way we approach life. A growth mindset, which views challenges as opportunities, empowers us, while a fixed mindset restricts our potential.
- **Actions:** The choices we make significantly influence our emotional well-being. Engaging in activities that reflect our values and passions brings a deeper sense of purpose and fulfilment.

By nurturing our inner world, we can cultivate a deep, enduring sense of well-being that transcends the changing tides of external circumstances.

THE SET POINT AND ITS INFLUENCE

Our genetics play a role in determining our baseline level of happiness, known as the "set point". While some people are naturally more optimistic and others more prone to pessimism, this set point is not a fixed destiny. Though genetics may set the stage, we are empowered to shift our outlook and elevate our happiness through intentional habits and practices.

THE CONDUCTOR WITHIN: HARMONISING YOUR INNER ORCHESTRA

Imagine your mind as a dynamic orchestra where your thoughts, emotions, and actions are like different instruments. Just as a skilled conductor brings harmony to diverse sounds, you have the ability to shape and balance your internal experience.

- **Thoughts:** These are the melodies you compose. By cultivating positive thought patterns, you create a harmonious symphony of well-being.
- **Emotions:** Like instruments, emotions require careful tuning. Balancing their expression is essential to maintaining a harmonious inner world.
- **Actions:** Like a conductor's baton, your actions direct the performance of your life. When they are in harmony with your values, they create a fulfilling and meaningful existence.

Compassionate Recovery: A Symphony of Self-Kindness

In the face of challenges like addiction or trauma, self-compassion becomes your most valuable instrument. It's the same as a warm-up exercise for your internal orchestra, creating the conditions for healing and growth. By understanding your unique composition and mastering the art of self-conduct, you can craft a life filled with joy, resilience, and purpose.

A Spiritual Path: Adding Depth to Your Symphony

Spiritual practices enrich your inner orchestra. Mindfulness, meditation, and connecting with nature introduce new instruments. These practices introduce peace, clarity, and purpose to the ensemble. These spiritual elements blend seamlessly with self-compassion, creating a symphony of healing, balance, and growth. By blending the art of self-compassion with the wisdom of spirituality, you can become the master conductor of your life. With every note, you have the power to create a masterpiece of resilience, hope, and fulfilment.

Reflective Questions Based on the "Conductor Within" Metaphor

- **Self-awareness and Inner Orchestration:** How well do you currently conduct your inner orchestra? Are your thoughts, emotions, and actions harmoniously aligned, or is there dissonance? What are the specific instruments (emotions) that need more attention in your orchestra?
- **Compassionate Self-Leadership:** In what ways can you promote greater self-compassion as the conductor of your life? How can you create a more supportive environment for your inner orchestra to thrive?
- **Spiritual Depth and Harmony:** How can you incorporate spiritual practices to enrich the composition of your life? What new instruments or harmonies could you introduce to your inner orchestra through spiritual exploration?
- **Action and Alignment:** How well do your current actions align with the symphony you desire to create? Are there specific actions you can take to bring your inner orchestra into greater harmony?
- **Overcoming Challenges:** When faced with life's challenges, how can you use the conductor metaphor to manage difficult emotions and thoughts? How can you maintain a sense of harmony and resilience during these times?

DISCOVERY OF THE INNER LIGHT: SPIRITUALITY AS A BEACON IN COMPASSIONATE RECOVERY

The human quest for healing and transformation is an ancient journey. It is not a pursuit for external approval. It is a path inward, where we uncover the radiant light that resides within. As Marcel Proust so beautifully expressed, "The real voyage of discovery consists not in seeking new landscapes but in having new eyes."

We should seek to see life's mysteries with a renewed perspective. In the context of Compassionate Recovery (CR), spirituality becomes more than a belief system – it transforms into a tool for rewriting your personal narrative. Rather than acting as a rigid framework of control, spirituality in CR embraces the inherent mysteries of life. It nurtures openness, curiosity, and a profound appreciation for life's ineffable beauty. It acknowledges that certain aspects of existence, much like the human spirit, transcend the bounds of logic and reason.

Through sacred practices like meditation, prayer, or simply spending time in nature, you engage with life as an evolving journey. These practices invite exploration, promote personal growth, and create a connection to something greater, whether that is the divine, a higher power, or the interconnectedness of all living things.

This connection to something larger serves as a powerful source of hope. Addiction often brings profound disconnection and separation from your true self and the world around you. Spirituality offers a bridge back to that sense of connection. It provides comfort during difficult times, reminding you that you are not alone in your struggles. It nurtures empathy, self-compassion, and acceptance, all essential ingredients for healing. The connection spirituality encourages extends beyond the self, guiding you toward supportive communities, whether in faith-based groups, recovery programmes, or deeper connections with loved ones. This sense of belonging is a powerful antidote to the isolation that often fuels addiction. Finding deeper meaning and purpose in these relationships helps guide you toward a life beyond addiction, filled with lasting fulfilment.

STEERING CLEAR OF SPIRITUAL BYPASSING: A COMPASS FOR AUTHENTIC GROWTH ON THE RECOVERY PATH

The journey of recovery is a quest for authenticity, a process of peeling back layers to uncover the truest version of yourself. However, this path can be fraught with detours, one of which is the alluring yet deceptive pitfall of spiritual bypassing. Spiritual bypassing involves using spiritual beliefs or practices as a shield to deflect difficult emotions, unresolved issues, or challenging situations. It represents the difference between processing pain and simply numbing it. Instead of fostering authentic growth, it becomes a defence mechanism that prevents you from confronting the inner turmoil crucial for lasting transformation.

Red Flags to Look Out For

1. Toxic Positivity

Ignoring negative emotions like sadness or anger and forcing a façade of constant happiness. These attitudes can create a culture where you feel ashamed of expressing your authentic feelings, leading to emotional suppression rather than a supportive environment for healing and understanding.

Example in Recovery: Focusing solely on the inspirational stories of others who have overcome addiction while refusing to acknowledge your own struggles or the hard work required for long-term sobriety. Toxic positivity from others can create shame when you experience negative emotions, making it important to recognise all feelings.

Examples:

"Just think happy thoughts!" – Encourages ignoring genuine feelings.

"It could be worse; just look on the bright side!" – Minimises legitimate struggles.

"Everything happens for a reason; just be grateful!" – Suggests overlooking pain.

"Don't worry, be happy!" – Implies that it's not okay to express negative feelings.

"You just need to let go of the negative!" – Suppresses instead of working through emotions.

"Smile! It's a beautiful day!" – Dismissive when someone is struggling.

"Anger is a waste of energy; just channel it into something positive." – Dismisses the validity of anger.

"Look at the glass half full!" – Pressures adopting a positive outlook.

"You should just be more positive; it's all about your mindset." – Suggests changing mindset without introspection.

"Why dwell on the negative when you can celebrate the positive?" – Promotes avoidance of emotions.

2. Empty Words

Using spiritual jargon or concepts to explain away problems without taking responsibility for actions. While these phrases can be comforting or inspiring, they may also serve to avoid addressing deeper issues or personal accountability.

Examples:

"Just raise your vibration, and everything will be fine."

"If you truly wanted it, you would manifest it."

"You just need to align your energy, and everything will fall into place."

"You must transcend the situation to see the bigger picture."

"Just let it go, and the universe will provide."

"Everything happens for a reason; think of it as a lesson."

"Just be present, and the past will no longer affect you."

"It's all about cosmic timing; trust the universe."

"We agreed to this experience before incarnating."

"Your higher self is guiding you; trust it instead of taking action."

3. The Blame Game

Masquerading self-centeredness or judgment as spiritual teachings by blaming others for your struggles. These phrases can obscure your own issues, placing blame on others instead of nurturing compassion and understanding.

Examples:

"If you're still struggling, you're just stuck in a victim mentality."

"This is all part of their karma; they brought this on themselves."

"Their low vibrations are affecting my energy; I need to distance myself. "

"I can't progress because I am surrounded by negative people."

"You need to take personal responsibility, as I have, instead of blaming your circumstances."

"They must be on a different soul journey, which is why they're in this situation."

"We're frequencies at odds; their struggles are why I feel stuck."

"This is a lesson in detachment from those who don't understand."

4. Spiritual Escapism

Using spiritual practices to avoid real-life challenges in recovery, such as attending support group meetings or therapy sessions. These behaviours can provide temporary relief but ultimately prevent you from addressing core issues.

Examples:

"I'm just going to meditate instead of dealing with these feelings."

"If I keep my thoughts positive, all my problems will disappear."

"I need to detach from all worldly problems and focus on my spiritual growth."

"I'll just pray for guidance instead of seeking professional help."

"I'll repeat affirmations to manifest a different life without addressing my current struggles."

"If I do my rituals every day, I won't need to attend therapy."

"I'm going on a retreat to escape my problems rather than facing them."

"I believe everything happens for a reason, so I don't need to change my situation."

"Once I reach enlightenment, all my issues will be resolved automatically."

"Buying spiritual books and crystals will somehow resolve my life challenges."

5. Dismissing Pain

Spiritual bypassers may downplay the seriousness of difficult emotions or experiences, brushing them aside with phrases like "focus on the positive." These phrases can inadvertently discourage healthy emotional processing and support.

Examples:

"Just let it go." – Suggests that someone should simply release their feelings without processing them.

"Everything happens for a reason." – Minimises pain by implying it's part of a bigger plan.

"You need to find the silver lining." – Encourages seeking positives without acknowledging pain.

"Focus on the light." – Dismisses the reality of difficult feelings.

"You'll be okay if you just raise your vibration." – Implies that spiritual energy alone can resolve suffering.

"Just keep your thoughts positive." – Suggests negative feelings are a choice.

"Don't be attached to outcomes." – Might dismiss genuine concerns or desires.

"You're creating your own reality." – Places blame for suffering on the individual without context.

"Seek gratitude in everything." – Can pressure you to feel grateful instead of grieving.

"Just trust the universe." – Downplays the need for practical action during tough times.

6. Minimising

Downplaying the seriousness of difficult emotions or experiences can leave you feeling ashamed or confused about your struggles.

Examples:

"It's not that big of a deal." – Suggests feelings are not worthy of concern.

"You'll get over it." – Implies emotions should be brushed aside.

"Others have it worse." – Compares struggles, invalidating personal pain.

"You're just being dramatic." – Accuses someone of exaggerating their feelings.

"You should just toughen up." – Suggests vulnerability isn't acceptable.

"It's all in your head." - Minimises struggles by implying they aren't real.

"You're fine; it's probably just a phase." – Belittles the depth of someone's feelings.

"Just think positive thoughts." – Implies thoughts alone can negate serious emotions.

"Don't worry; it'll work itself out." – Suggests avoidance instead of confrontation.

"You need a thicker skin." – Encourages less sensitivity instead of validating emotions.

7. **Spiritual Condescension**

Believing oneself to be on a higher spiritual plane can manifest as judgment or lack of empathy for those struggling in recovery. This attitude can create an environment where you feel judged rather than supported.

Examples:

"I've evolved past that." – Dismisses others' struggles as less valid.

"You're still attached to the material world." – Suggests a lack of spiritual understanding in others.

"You need to raise your consciousness." – Implies others are less aware.

"I don't have time for negativity." – Refuses to engage with others' pain.

"If you really meditated, you wouldn't feel this way." – Blames struggles on incorrect practices.

"You must be manifesting this situation." – Attributes challenges to others' perceived failures.

"You're just not ready for the truth." – Positions oneself as more enlightened than others.

"You need to do the inner work." – Can sound judgmental about others' efforts.

Why Critical Thinking Matters in Spiritual Bypassing

Let's look at the following quote from Byron Katie as an example of why critical thinking is important when identifying spiritual bypassing:

If I had a prayer, it would be this: "God, spare me from the desire for love, approval, and appreciation. Amen."

Byron Katie is the founder of Byron Katie International, an organisation that encompasses the School for The Work and Turnaround House, based in Ojai, California. Recognised by Time magazine as a spiritual innovator for the 21st century, she continues to inspire transformative change through her teachings.

Byron Katie's quote can be interpreted in two ways:

An Argument FOR Spiritual Bypassing

- **Neglecting Core Needs:** Love, approval, and appreciation are fundamental human needs. Completely eliminating the desire for them might be seen as denying a core part of the human experience.
- **Focus on Negativity:** The prayer is based on the need to be "spared" from these desires, suggesting a struggle with them rather than seeking a more balanced approach.
- **Eliminating Desires:** It's important to acknowledge that some might interpret this quote as promoting spiritual bypassing by focusing solely on eliminating desires rather than achieving a balanced and healthy relationship with them.

Arguments AGAINST Spiritual Bypassing

- **Non-Attachment vs. Denial:** The quote might be advocating for non-attachment to external validation, not denying the emotions themselves. It could be a desire for self-worth to come from within, not from external sources.
- **Focus on Self-reliance:** The prayer could be interpreted as a plea for inner strength and the ability to find fulfilment without needing approval from others.
- **Healthy Non-Attachment:** Healthy non-attachment acknowledges and accepts the desire for love, approval, and appreciation as natural human emotions. It's about not letting those desires control your behaviour or define your self-worth. You can strive to fulfil those needs in healthy ways without becoming dependent on external validation.

Understanding the Context

To truly understand the quote's meaning, it's helpful to consider the context in which it was said. Here are some questions to ponder:

- Was Byron Katie speaking from a place of personal struggle?
- Was she referencing a specific situation?
- Did she have a broader philosophy about these desires?

Context: Byron Katie's method, *The Work*, focuses on questioning negative thoughts and beliefs. Understanding the context of Katie's work, which emphasises questioning negative thought patterns, sheds light on her intention behind the quote. Perhaps she's suggesting that the desire for external validation can stem from negative beliefs about ourselves, and through self-inquiry, we can find a more secure sense of self-worth.

Critical thinking is essential when evaluating spiritual teachings to avoid spiritual bypassing. Byron Katie's quote can either be interpreted as encouraging non-attachment or as denying core human needs, depending on the lens through which it's viewed. By questioning both the potential for bypassing and the pursuit of inner self-reliance, we can create a more balanced understanding. It's important to examine the context and intent behind such teachings, ensuring that we don't confuse healthy non-attachment with avoidance of natural emotional desires. Critical thinking helps us engage with these ideas in a grounded, insightful way.

The New Age Maze: Critical Thinking as Your Guide

The mind-body-spirit movement offers a wealth of tools for self-discovery, but understanding this landscape requires a discerning eye. Indiscriminating acceptance of any philosophy, new age or otherwise, is discouraged, as many overlook the complexity of human experience and the ever-evolving nature of knowledge. Worse yet, some exploit this openness to peddle pseudoscience, magical thinking, and quick fixes that can endanger well-being. To navigate this terrain safely, you need a compass which should be a balance between critical thinking and ethical integrity. Critical thinking empowers you to discern evidence-based practices from unsubstantiated claims. Ethical considerations ensure that any new philosophy promotes personal growth without exploiting vulnerabilities. This means maintaining a healthy scepticism towards charismatic leaders and their grandiose promises.

The pursuit of self-discovery can veer off course when taken to extremes. Dismissing conventional medicine entirely in favour of unproven alternative therapies can be dangerous. Furthermore, some mind-body-spirit groups exhibit cult-like behaviours, manipulating followers and causing psychological and financial harm. While alternative and holistic approaches offer valuable tools, approaching them with tempered scepticism is crucial. Seek guidance from reputable sources, maintain open communication with loved ones, and prioritise evidence-based methodologies. This balanced approach allows you to harness the potential of alternative philosophies while avoiding hidden pitfalls.

Psychedelics and the Spiritual Seeker: A Call for Prudence

The recent surge in research and interest in psychedelics as tools for transformation is exciting but calls for careful consideration. While clinical trials highlight their therapeutic potential, it is essential to approach these substances within supervised, controlled environments due to safety concerns and legal limitations. Although psychedelics generally have a low risk of addiction, they can still present significant dangers, particularly for people with vulnerabilities or pre-existing mental health conditions.

Potential Risks to Consider

- **Psychosis:** People with a predisposition to schizophrenia or bipolar disorder may experience psychotic or manic episodes.
- **Exacerbated Symptoms:** Studies indicate that psychedelics can worsen symptoms in people with bipolar disorder.
- **Triggering Latent Conditions:** Anecdotal evidence suggests psychedelics may trigger dormant mental health issues.
- **Limited Research:** The safety profile for people with pre-existing medical conditions like heart disease is unclear due to limited research.

Recovery is a multi-faceted journey that demands ongoing commitment and professional guidance. It's not a one-time psychedelic encounter. True healing necessitates sustained effort and comprehensive support systems, not the allure of a quick fix. Psychedelics hold promise, but their use requires careful consideration, especially for those with underlying vulnerabilities. Embrace a cautious approach, prioritising safety and informed decision-making as you navigate the path towards holistic well-being.

Reflective Questions: The New Age Maze

- **Personal Exploration:** How do you balance your openness to new ideas and experiences with a healthy scepticism? What criteria do you use to evaluate the credibility of alternative approaches?
- **Ethical Considerations:** In what ways can you contribute to a more ethical and informed mind-body-spirit community? How can you protect yourself and others from potential exploitation or harm?
- **Informed Decision Making:** How do you determine which alternative therapies or practices align with your personal values and health goals? What role does evidence-based research play in your decision-making process?

- **Community and Support:** How can you cultivate a supportive community that encourages both open-mindedness and critical thinking? What role do you play in helping others navigate the complexities of the mind-body-spirit landscape?
- **Personal Growth:** How can you integrate the best aspects of the mind-body-spirit movement into your life while maintaining a grounded and balanced perspective? What strategies can you employ to prevent falling into the traps of extremism or magical thinking?

WALKING ALONGSIDE EQUALS: AN EGALITARIAN APPROACH TO COMPASSIONATE RECOVERY

"Compassion is not a relationship between the healer and the wounded. It's a relationship between equals. Only when we know our own darkness well can we be present in the darkness of others. Compassion becomes real when we recognise our shared humanity."

– Pema Chödrön

In the realm of Compassionate Recovery (CR), whether from addiction, trauma, or any form of suffering, the concept of compassion is imperative. Pema Chödrön's profound insight encapsulates the core of CR, representing a radical departure from traditional healing models. Unlike hierarchical approaches that position helpers above those seeking help, CR promotes a dynamic of equality. This shift challenges the notion of "fixing" broken people, emphasising instead mutual understanding, empathy, and shared humanity. True healing emerges from a space of authenticity and vulnerability. As Chödrön suggests, recognising and embracing our own shadows enables us to authentically connect with and support others on their journeys.

You are not a passive recipient but an active agent in your healing process, whether you are seeking recovery or offering support. You are valued equally, presenting unique perspectives and strengths. This egalitarian framework empowers you to reclaim agency and ownership over your well-being. CR cultivates a safe, non-judgemental space where you can feel seen, heard, and understood.

By acknowledging your shared struggles, you build trust and authenticity, encouraging others to do the same. Within this environment of empathy and mutual support, you confront challenges, heal, and ultimately thrive. This transformative approach transcends traditional power dynamics. It invites us to walk side by side, sharing experiences and supporting each other. Through this collective journey of self-discovery and compassion, true healing and transformation become possible.

BOOK RECOMMENDATIONS

Here are some book recommendations on nurturing well-being through internal exploration:

- ***Man's Search for Meaning*** by Viktor E. Frankl is a classic memoir by a Holocaust survivor and explores the importance of finding meaning in life, even in the face of extreme suffering.
- ***The Power of Now*** by Eckhart Tolle teaches readers how to live in the present moment and find peace of mind.
- ***Daring Greatly*** by Brené Brown explores the importance of vulnerability and courage in living a wholehearted life.
- ***Insight Meditation*** by Joseph Goldstein is a wonderful introduction to Vipassana meditation, a form of mindfulness meditation that can help you develop self-awareness and inner peace.
- ***Wherever You Go, There You Are*** by Jon Kabat-Zinn is another great introduction to mindfulness meditation, and it also includes exercises that you can use to practise mindfulness in your daily life.

CHAPTER 8 - METAMORPHOSIS: EMBRACING CHANGE WITH SELF-COMPASSION

The journey of overcoming addiction can be compared to the remarkable transformation of a caterpillar into a butterfly. It is a process of shedding old limitations and embracing new life with resilience and grace. Just as a caterpillar transforms within its chrysalis and emerges as a vibrant butterfly, you undergo an astonishing metamorphosis to heal and flourish. While programmes like the 12-step model have offered valuable support to many, recovery is inherently personal and may require a tailored approach. CR offers an empowering alternative that prioritises mindfulness, self-compassion, and personal growth.

At the heart of CR is a shift from self-condemnation to self-kindness. Complementing more structured approaches, CR embraces the diverse nature of your experiences. Creating a nurturing environment grounded in compassion that empowers you to embark on a deeply personal healing journey. This process is embracing flexibility, growth, and resilience.

THE POWER OF CHANGE: A FAMILIAR FRIEND IN DISGUISE

Your path through Compassionate Recovery goes beyond simply overcoming unhealthy coping strategies. It initiates an incredible transformation, enabling you to break free from the constraints of your past and embrace a lively future. Like a caterpillar transforming into a beautiful butterfly, you have the innate strength and potential to rise above your challenges and emerge as a revitalised and empowered person.

As a certified Martha Beck coach, I suggest that with the combination of Martha Beck's Change Cycle and Compassionate Recovery, you can embark on a metamorphic journey to discover your wings and soar. Change is an inevitable companion no matter where you are on your recovery path. The change cycle ignites when the once-comforting familiarity of your former self begins to feel constricting, even suffocating. A yearning emerges to break free from a limited, repetitive existence that no longer nourishes your well-being or sparks joy. Or perhaps, like a contented caterpillar immersed in its leafy realm, you may find comfort in your current life, inching forward on a well-worn path. Yet beneath this tranquil exterior, an intense restlessness stirs. A yearning to metamorphose, to shed the confines of the known and embrace the uncharted, awakens within you. While filled with uncertainty, this transition holds the promise of hidden wings ready to spread wide and soar. The transformative process is explained below.

DEATH AND REBIRTH: ENTERING THE CHRYSALIS

The caterpillar's journey ends dramatically by becoming a chrysalis. This occurs when the life of the caterpillar becomes unsustainable, much like your own when addictive behaviour becomes unmanageable. In Martha Beck's Cycle, this is called "death and rebirth". The caterpillar transitions to a chrysalis, where an incredible process unfolds. Its familiar form dissolves. This is a powerful metaphor for letting go of the old ways that no longer serve us. In this initial phase, you learn to abstain from addictive behaviours while identifying and addressing past experiences, limiting beliefs, and habits that no longer benefit or serve you.

Its introspective phase presents a chance to eradicate the behaviours that have been holding you back. This can be uncomfortable, but just as the caterpillar's transformation is necessary for flight, letting go of this limited identity is essential for growth. This dissolving process is just the beginning, though. As we delve deeper, we'll explore the stages of change inspired by the butterfly's journey. We'll discover how to navigate challenges, embrace opportunities, and finally emerge, ready to take flight as the beautiful butterfly you were always meant to be.

Practical Strategies for the Stage of Death and Rebirth: Entering the Chrysalis

This stage is about transformation: Letting go of past shame and embracing a new, empowered version of yourself. Below are some practical strategies designed to guide you through this pivotal phase.

1) Acknowledgement and Acceptance: Shedding Shame and Embracing Your Story

The journey begins with honest acknowledgement. Recognise that addiction is a part of your life narrative - one chapter among many - not the entirety of who you are. This is about accepting the reality of your experience. By acknowledging your struggles without judgment, you can begin to let go of the shame that has weighed you down. Embracing your story means accepting both the painful and the transformative aspects of your past, which in turn opens up space for healing and growth.

2) The Starting Point: Recognising Addiction Without Self-Blame

The first step in this transformation is to face the truth about your addiction. This recognition is a powerful and necessary act, not one of self-condemnation but of clarity and honesty. Addiction, while a significant part of your story, does not define your entire identity. Understanding this helps you see the situation objectively, setting the stage for meaningful change. This perspective allows you to focus on the actions needed to overcome the challenges rather than getting caught in a cycle of guilt and regret.

3) Self-Compassion as Your Inner Ally

Cultivating self-compassion is essential during this stage of rebirth. Think of it as extending the same kindness and understanding to yourself that you would offer a close friend in need. Self-compassion involves challenging your inner critic and replacing harsh self-judgment with nurturing support. This shift in perspective reinforces your inherent worthiness of healing and personal growth. By treating yourself with compassion, you create a safe space for vulnerability and resilience, which is crucial for long-term recovery.

4) Mindfulness: Cultivating Awareness for Empowered Choices and Seeking Clarity

Mindfulness is a cornerstone of this transformation process. By developing a non-judgmental awareness of your thoughts, emotions, and physical sensations, you gain invaluable insights into your inner world. This practice helps you observe cravings and triggers without automatically reacting to them. Instead, you learn to make conscious choices that support your recovery. Engaging in structured mindfulness practices, such as working through The 12 Stepping Stones Companion Guide, can further enhance your clarity and emotional balance, empowering you to navigate the challenges of recovery with greater ease.

Exploring the Roots: Unearthing Underlying Causes

Addiction isn't an isolated issue. CR delves deeper, exploring the emotional, psychological, social, and environmental factors that may have contributed to its development. This involves dedicated self-reflection to address past traumas, unresolved emotions, and unhealthy coping mechanisms. By understanding the "why" behind your addiction, you can develop more effective strategies for lasting change.

Building Your Toolkit: Essential Practices for Recovery

- **Self-Reflection:** Journaling, meditation, therapy, coaching, and/or counselling can be invaluable tools to explore your past experiences and identify emotional triggers.
- **Mindfulness in Action:** Staying present and aware in the moment allows you to focus on your intention to heal and grow.
- **Acknowledge and Accept:** Recognise the impact of past experiences without judgement. This is explored through The Four Cardinal Directions.
- **Seek Support:** Building a strong support system is crucial. Get in touch with a therapist, mentor, coach, or support group who can offer guidance, encouragement, and a sense of belonging.
- **Embrace Vulnerability and Authenticity:** Change often requires stepping outside your comfort zone. Embrace vulnerability and authenticity as an opportunity for growth. Be open to new experiences and perspectives.
- **Manage Emotions:** Learn healthy coping mechanisms to manage difficult emotions.

Reflection Prompts for Death and Rebirth: Entering the Chrysalis

Phase	Reflection Prompts	Take a Moment to Reflect
Acknowledgement and Acceptance	• Reflect on how you currently perceive addiction in your life. Are there any feelings of shame or guilt attached to it? • How might acknowledging addiction without self-blame impact your journey towards recovery?	
Self-Compassion	• Think about how you typically treat yourself when facing challenges. How can you cultivate more self-compassion in your recovery journey? • Consider instances where you've been overly self-critical. How can you reframe these thoughts with kindness and understanding?	

Mindfulness	• Reflect on your current level of awareness regarding your thoughts, emotions, and triggers related to addiction. How can incorporating mindfulness practices into your daily routine help you make empowered choices in your recovery process?	
Exploring the Roots	• Take some time to delve into the underlying causes of your addiction. Are there any past traumas or unresolved emotions contributing to it? • How do you think understanding the root causes of your addiction can impact your approach to recovery?	
Building Your Toolkit	• Consider which self-reflection practices resonate with you the most. How can you incorporate them into your daily life? • Reflect on the role of vulnerability in your recovery journey. How can embracing vulnerability lead to growth and transformation?	

Managing Emotions	• Identify some of the emotions that tend to trigger addictive behaviours for you. How can you develop healthier coping mechanisms to manage these emotions? • Reflect on the importance of seeking support from others in your recovery process. Who can you turn to for guidance, encouragement, and understanding?	

DREAMING AND SCHEMING: BIRTHING POTENTIAL WITHIN THE CHRYSALIS

- **The Chrysalis: The Place Where Dreams are Born**

Inside the chrysalis, a transformation unfolds. The frenetic energy of the caterpillar's life dissolves, replaced by a profound stillness. But this isn't dormancy – it's a vessel of creation. The seemingly formless soup is a potent brew of possibility.

- **Dreaming Big: Birthing Your Vision**

Here, the blueprint for the butterfly begins to take shape. Delicate wings, once unimaginable, develop. This mirrors your own transformation. Just as the butterfly dreams within the chrysalis, you, too, can envision a future free from the limitations of active addiction. The chrysalis stage allows you to delve into the recesses of your mind. Perhaps you see yourself in a new, fulfilling career, surrounded by supportive relationships, or contributing to a cause you deeply care about. Whatever your aspirations, this is the time to nurture them with hope and possibility.

- **Scheming for Success: Bridging the Gap**

Dreaming isn't enough. This stage, which Martha Beck named "dreaming and scheming", is also about strategic planning. Imagine sketching out a roadmap to your desired future. Brainstorm ideas, research resources, explore possibilities, and learn new strategies. This is where audacious dreams meet action, the fertile ground where your transformation takes root. Remember, the butterfly doesn't emerge overnight. It is a gradual process, a delicate dance between dreaming and scheming. Embrace the tranquillity within the chrysalis as the potential for your transformation takes flight.

- **Practical Strategies for the Stage of Dreaming and Scheming**

  - **Letting Go:** Forgive yourself and others, and release attachments to old habits and identities.
  - **Mindfulness:** Maintain mindfulness practices to stay present and focused on your intentions.
  - **Reflection:** Reflect on your new awareness, skills, and tools you have acquired so far.
  - **Exploration:** Discover new interests, activities, and perspectives that align with a healthier life.
  - **Vision Boarding:** Create a visual representation of your aspirations and goals to solidify your vision for the future.
  - **Goal Setting:** Establish achievable short-term goals aligned with your recovery and values.
  - **Creative Expression:** Explore emotions and aspirations through creative outlets like art, writing and/or music.
  - **Community Engagement:** Connect with supportive friends, mentors, therapists, or recovery groups for encouragement and shared experiences.
  - **Self-Compassion:** Be kind to yourself throughout this exploration, acknowledging setbacks as natural parts of the process.

Reflection Prompts for Dreaming and Scheming: Birthing Potential Within the Chrysalis

Phase	Reflection Prompts	Take a Moment to Reflect
Dreaming Big – Birthing Your Vision	• Take a moment to envision your life beyond addiction. What does your ideal future look like? Consider aspects such as a career, relationships, personal growth, and your contribution to society. Reflect on the emotions and sensations that arise as you imagine this future. How does it feel to embrace the possibility of transformation and growth?	
Scheming for Success – Bridging the Gap	• Think about concrete steps you can take to turn your dreams into reality. What resources, skills, or support systems do you need to achieve your vision? • Consider any barriers or challenges that may arise along the way. How can you proactively address these obstacles and stay committed to your goals?	

Embracing the Process	• Reflect on the metaphor of the chrysalis as a cocoon of tranquillity where transformation occurs. How can you create moments of stillness and reflection in your own life to nurture your dreams and aspirations? Consider the balance between dreaming and taking action. How can you cultivate patience and perseverance as you work towards your desired future?	
Celebrating Progress	• Take stock of any progress you've already made towards your goals, no matter how small. How does acknowledging your achievements motivate you to continue moving forward? • Reflect on the importance of self-compassion and resilience in the face of setbacks or challenges. How can you maintain a positive mindset and stay focused on your long-term vision?	

THE HERO'S EMERGENCE: PREPARING TO TAKE FLIGHT

The chrysalis glistens, a quiet testament to the transformation taking place inside. A shudder passes through it, and then, with a courageous effort, a butterfly breaks free. Its wings, once ethereal dreams swirling in a shapeless mass, are now a vivid reality. This is the hero's emergence, a pivotal chapter in your transformation. You've dissolved your old self and stand poised for an incredible take-off. But your wings, symbolising your new-found skills and perspectives, are fragile and require immense effort to unfurl.

Just as the butterfly painstakingly pumps fluid into its crumpled wings, allowing them to dry and strengthen in the sun's warmth, your recovery journey will take time and present challenges and temptations. The familiar allure of your old ways might beckon you back. Setbacks may occur, leaving you discouraged and your wings feeling heavy and stifled once more. In these times, remember the resilience you cultivated during the introspective chrysalis stage. This newfound strength will be your compass, guiding you through the inevitable storms. Doubts will arise, but with each conquered challenge, your wings will grow stronger. With each setback, you'll learn valuable lessons, refining your ability to navigate the currents of change.

The hero's emergence is a dance between exhilaration and struggle. The journey is about conquering mountains and exploring valleys. This is a tribute to the human spirit's ability to rise above adversity. Embrace the challenges, for they are the very forces that will strengthen your wings and propel you towards a future brimming with purpose and freedom. Just like the butterfly, with perseverance and unwavering determination, you will take flight, soaring above the limitations of your past and embracing the limitless possibilities that lie ahead. CR empowers you to not just survive and overcome addiction but to thrive.

Practical strategies for the stage of the Hero's Emergence: Taking Flight with Renewed Strength

Recovery is a continuous journey of self-discovery and personal evolution. This stage focuses on integrating the lessons and tools acquired throughout your journey into your everyday life. Here's how:

- **Living Your Values:** Integrate the values you discovered throughout recovery into your daily choices and actions. What truly matters to you? How can you live a life that reflects these values?
- **Cultivating Compassion:** Maintain a practice of self-compassion. You are worthy of kindness and understanding, even on challenging days. Extend this compassion to others as well.
- **Mindfulness in Action:** Continue to practise mindfulness. By staying present and aware, you can respond to challenges with clarity and avoid impulsive reactions. The RAIN technique, a powerful tool for radical acceptance, can be particularly helpful during challenging times.
- **Resilience for Life's Ups and Downs:** Embrace adversity as an opportunity for growth. You've developed resilience through recovery. Now, use it to navigate life's inevitable challenges with strength and wisdom.

Maintaining Your Well-being: A Toolkit for Long-Term Success

- **Mindfulness and Acceptance:** Practise mindful acceptance and address challenges in a non-judgemental way. Respond with clarity and avoid impulsive reactions.
- **Manage Your Emotions:** Utilise healthy coping mechanisms to manage difficult emotions that may arise.
- **Seek Support:** Lean on your support system for encouragement and accountability.
- **Self-reflect:** Regularly evaluate triggers, patterns, and underlying issues to inform adjustments in your recovery plan.
- **Be Adaptable:** Embrace flexibility in response to unexpected events, viewing challenges as opportunities for growth.
- **Reassess Goals:** Revisit and adjust goals as needed to maintain direction and purpose even in the face of adversity.
- **Forgive Yourself:** Cultivate self-compassion and forgiveness, understanding that recovery is a journey of progress and setbacks.

***Remember:** Compassionate recovery is a transformative gift you give yourself. By embracing its principles, you can build lasting resilience, cultivate self-compassion, and live a life filled with purpose, authenticity, and fulfilment. You are not just overcoming addiction – you are creating a life that is truly your own.

Reflection Prompts for The Hero's Emergence: Taking Flight with Renewed Strength

Phases	Reflection Prompts	Take a Moment to Reflect
Embracing Challenges	• Reflect on a recent setback or challenge you faced in your recovery journey. How did you respond to it? What lessons did you learn from the experience? • Consider the metaphor of the new butterfly's struggle to unfurl its wings. How does this resonate with your journey of overcoming obstacles and strengthening your resilience?	

Living Your Values	• Take some time to revisit the values you discovered throughout your recovery process. How have these values shaped your decisions and actions in daily life? • Reflect on ways to align your actions more closely with your core values moving forward. What steps can you take to live a life that reflects what truly matters to you?	
Cultivating Compassion	• Think about moments when you've been hard on yourself during challenging times. How can you extend more compassion and kindness to yourself, especially during moments of struggle? • Consider ways you can show compassion towards others who may be facing similar challenges in their own journeys. How can you offer support and understanding to those around you?	

Mindfulness in Action	• Reflect on how mindfulness practices have helped you stay present and aware throughout your recovery journey. How can you continue to incorporate mindfulness into your daily life to maintain clarity and focus? • Consider specific situations where practising mindfulness has helped you respond to challenges more effectively. How can you apply these insights to future situations?	
Maintaining Your Well-being	• Take inventory of the healthy coping mechanisms and support systems you've relied on during difficult times. How can you continue to prioritise your well-being moving forward? Reflect on the importance of adaptability in navigating life's ups and downs. How can you embrace flexibility and resilience as you encounter unexpected events or setbacks?	

SOARING WITH WINGS OF TRANSFORMATION: THE PROMISED LAND

The golden sun bathes the landscape in warmth, casting a spotlight on the newly emerged butterfly. Its wings, once crumpled symbols of vulnerability, have undergone a miraculous transformation. Now, iridescent and vibrant, they shimmer like stained glass, each delicate vein tracing the map of its extraordinary journey. With a trembling breath, the butterfly opens its wings, marvelling at the newfound strength they possess. This is the promised land, the culmination of your metamorphosis. Everything has been worth it, as each challenge, moment of introspection, and quiet dream, along with the planning within your chrysalis, has led you to this very place. As you tentatively take your first flight, exhilaration flows over you. The world unfolds beneath you, a breathtaking landscape of lively colours and endless possibilities.

Embrace your transformed self. You are no longer the caterpillar confined to a myopic existence of munching leaves but a radiant butterfly capable of soaring to unimaginable heights. You've discovered a new-found purpose, a vision for your future that resonates deep within your being. You've dissolved the constricting behaviours of your past and emerged as a beautiful expression of your authentic self.

Perhaps the most important aspect of the promised land is the new-found sense of belonging. You see the world through transformed eyes, recognising the beauty and potential that surrounds you. You connect with others who have embarked on their own journeys of change, forming a supportive community that celebrates your growth. This promised land is a state of being, a place of peace, and a deep understanding that you possess the inner strength and resilience to face whatever life presents. You've tasted the freedom of flight, and you'll never settle for crawling again.

Just like the butterfly, you, too, have the potential to shed your limitations and emerge as your most authentic self. Embrace the inevitable cycles of change, for they are the catalysts for growth and self-discovery. With courage and perseverance, you can navigate your unique journey, reaching a place of peace, purpose, and unwavering confidence to take flight whenever the winds of change stir.

Practical strategies for the stage of the Promised Land

- **Celebrating Milestones: Marking Your Path to Success**

Take time to acknowledge and celebrate your victories, both big and small. Every milestone, every achievement, and every day you choose health and well-being over addictive behavioural patterns is a tribute to your strength and resilience. Celebrate these moments with loved ones, reward yourself for reaching goals, and allow the sense of accomplishment to fuel your continued motivation.

- **Cultivating Gratitude: Appreciation Encourages Abundance**

Gratitude is a powerful tool for cultivating a positive outlook and sense of well-being. Be grateful for the progress you've made, the support you've received, and the opportunities for growth and transformation you've encountered. Reflect on the challenges you've overcome and appreciate your inner strength.

- **Connecting with Purpose: Living a Life of Value**

CR opens doors to rediscover your values and passions. Reflect on what truly matters to you. Consider what ignites your spirit. Identify ways to contribute to the world and live a purpose-driven life aligned with your authentic self. Volunteer your time and pursue a lifelong dream. Find ways to make a positive impact on your community.

- **Building Supportive Relationships: A Circle of Strength**

Surround yourself with positive and supportive people who share your values and goals. Nurture authentic connections with loved ones, recovery groups, or mentors who offer encouragement and a sense of belonging. These networks are essential for creating feelings of joy, fulfilment, support and connection.

- **Embracing Your Creative Spirit: Unlocking Your Inner Artist**

Engage in activities that spark your creativity and allow you to express yourself. These activities could include art, music, writing, woodwork, gardening, or any other form of creative exploration. These activities nourish the soul, bring joy, and offer healthy outlets for emotions.

- **Mindfulness and Presence: Savouring the Journey**

Continue to cultivate mindfulness and presence in your daily life. Savour the present moment, find joy in simple pleasures and appreciate the beauty that surrounds you. Let go of worries about the past or anxieties about the future. By staying present, you can experience life to the fullest.

- **Continued Self-Reflection: A Lifelong Path of Growth**

Embrace ongoing self-reflection and personal growth. Remain curious about yourself and the world around you. Be open to new experiences, learning, insights, and opportunities that further your journey of recovery and self-discovery. Growth is a lifelong process, and CR equips you with the tools to navigate it with grace and self-acceptance.

Reflection Prompts for Soaring with Wings of Transformation: The Promised Land

Phase	Reflection Prompts	Take a Moment to Reflect
Celebrating Milestones	• Reflect on a recent accomplishment or milestone in your recovery journey. How did you celebrate this achievement? How did it make you feel? • Consider other milestones you hope to achieve in the future. How can you celebrate these moments and use them to fuel your continued motivation?	
Cultivating Gratitude	• Take a moment to express gratitude for the progress you've made in your recovery journey. What are you most grateful for right now? • Reflect on how practising gratitude has influenced your mindset and sense of well-being. How can you continue to promote gratitude in your daily life?	
Connecting with Purpose	• Think about activities or pursuits that bring meaning and purpose to your life. How do these align with your values and passions? • Reflect on ways you can contribute to the world and make a positive impact, both within your community and beyond.	

Building Supportive Relation-ships	• Consider the people in your life who have supported you on your journey of recovery. How have these relationships helped you grow and thrive? Reflect on ways you can nurture and strengthen these supportive connec-tions moving forward. How can you offer support to others who may be on their own paths of transformation?	
Embracing Your Cre-ative Spirit	• Reflect on the role of creativity in your recovery journey. How have creative activities helped you express yourself and cope with challenges? • Think about ways you can continue to engage in creative pursuits that bring you joy and fulfilment. How can you incorporate more creativi-ty into your daily life?	

Mindful-ness and Presence	• Reflect on moments when you've felt truly present and mindful in your daily life. What activities or practices help you promote mind-fulness? • Consider how staying present can enhance your experience of life and deepen your sense of grati-tude and connection.	
Continued Self-Reflection	• Take some time to reflect on how you've grown and evolved throughout your recovery journey. What insights have you gained about yourself? • Consider areas where you still have room for growth and devel-opment. How can you continue to embrace self-reflection as a tool for personal transformation?	

Remember, compassionate recovery moves in a cycle, not a linear path. As you navigate your recovery journey, you may revisit earlier stages as new challenges or opportunities arise. This is a natural part of growth. Embrace the journey, celebrate your progress, and trust that with each step, you are becoming the magnificent being you were always meant to be.

RESOURCES AVAILABLE ON COMPASSIONATE RECOVERY AND ADDICTION RECOVERY

- ***The Compassionate-Mind Guide to Recovering from Trauma and PTSD*** by Deborah A. Poole explores self-compassion as a key tool in healing from trauma, which can be a significant underlying factor in addiction.
- ***Self-Compassion: The Proven Power of Being Kind to Yourself*** by Kristin Neff is a core text on self-compassion, a practice emphasised throughout compassionate recovery.
- ***The Body Keeps the Score: Brain, Mind, and Body in the Healing of Trauma*** by Bessel van der Kolk explores the physical and emotional effects of trauma, a potential underlying factor in addiction.
- ***www.marthabeck.com***: This website is based on Martha Beck's teachings. She created and established the Change Cycle as a core concept used in compassionate recovery. While it doesn't directly address addiction, it explores personal growth and transformation.

CHAPTER 9 - CHANNEL YOUR INNER WAYFINDER: THE 8 CS OF SELF - LEADERSHIP

CRISIS CULTIVATES OPPORTUNITY

When life feels like it's crumbling around you and your old ways seem to be failing, the pain of crisis can be the catalyst for compassionate recovery. The Chinese character for "crisis" (危机 - wēijī) beautifully expresses this experience.

The dual nature of this word illustrates the incredible transformation possible through compassionate recovery (CR).

The first character (危 - wēi) means danger or instability, reflecting the immediate threat of a crisis. It signifies the upheaval and uncertainty that accompanies critical moments in life. The feeling of danger is often the catalyst that brings about a sense of urgency, compelling you to seek change. This immediate threat can be destabilising, yet it is within this very instability that the seeds of transformation are sown.

Inside each of us are the seeds of healing, waiting to be nurtured with compassion, love, trust, wisdom, and patience. In cultivating these seeds, we grow into embodiments of resilience and enlightenment.

The second character, (机 - jī), signifies opportunity. This element of the word emphasises that within the turmoil of a crisis, there is also the potential for growth and transformation. A crisis, while undeniably challenging, can also be the doorway to new possibilities and directions. This inherent duality within the word "crisis" perfectly aligns with the core principles of CR, which emphasise finding strength and positive change even amidst struggles.

In CR, we don't shy away from the harsh realities of addiction. We recognise that the crisis you face is a turning point, a moment where everything familiar crumbles. The path forward feels uncertain, but within this vulnerability lies the potential for immense growth. Just as the character "jī" signifies a turning point, CR teaches you to see this crisis as a springboard, propelling you towards a transformed life. The emphasis on compassion in "wēijī" speaks directly to the heart of CR. The danger inherent in a crisis exposes your vulnerabilities, leaving you feeling raw and bare. CR appears precisely at this moment of vulnerability, offering a safe space for healing. Through this process, you learn to practise empathy and understanding and develop a sense of connection.

Crisis, as a transformative force, highlights that challenges are part of the shared human experience. Recognising this dismantles isolation and shame, promoting connection and support. The concept of 危机 reminds you that even in hardship, positive change is possible. By embracing compassion and seeing crisis as a growth opportunity, you become empowered to overcome addiction and reclaim your life.

Reflective Prompt: The Transformative Potential of Crisis

- Consider the dual nature of "wēijī" (crisis) as both danger and opportunity.
- How can viewing crises through this lens change your approach to challenges?
- Write about a specific instance where a crisis led to unexpected positive changes or growth.

THE 8 CS OF SELF-LEADERSHIP

Developing your core self is essential for healing and recovery. We begin this journey by practising the 8 C's of Self-Leadership. The 8 Cs of Leadership framework was popularised by Dr. John C. Maxwell, a well-known author and speaker on leadership.

Definition	Key Aspect	Practical Impact	How to Cultivate
Calmness			
This refers to the ability to remain centred and composed, even in stressful situations. Calmness is essential for emotional regulation and inner stability. It enables us to respond to situations with clarity and mindfulness rather than reacting impulsively.	Achieve emotional stability and promote a sense of inner peace.	Enjoy improved decision-making, reduced stress, healthier relationships, and enhanced overall well-being.	• Boundary-Setting: Establishing and maintaining healthy boundaries can protect your emotional well-being and create a sense of safety. • Companion guide: Practising the 12 Stepping Stones - A Path to Wholeness: Engaging with these foundational practices can help you navigate your healing journey and cultivate a greater sense of calm. • Mindfulness Meditation: Regular mindfulness practices allow you to observe your thoughts and emotions without judgement, creating a deeper sense of calm and self-awareness. • Deep Breathing: Simple deep breathing exercises can effectively reduce stress and anxiety, promoting a sense of tranquillity in challenging situations. Yoga and Tai Chi: These practices blend physical movement with mindfulness, helping to calm both the mind and body while enhancing physical flexibility and strength. • Spending Time in Nature: Connecting with the natural world can have a profound calming effect on your mind and body, allowing for reflection and rejuvenation.

Clarity			
Clarity entails seeing situations as they are. Clarity involves seeing yourself, others, and situations without the distortions that arise from fears, judgements, or past trauma. When different emotions are activated, they can cloud our perception, making it hard to see things objectively.	Clarity is about recognising these emotions without letting them dominate your perspective. Clarity allows you to step back and understand what's happening with openness and honesty. You're not overwhelmed by your feelin gs or stuck in your stories about how things "should" be.	With clarity, you can evaluate situations, relationships, and decisions more effectively. You avoid reactive responses and instead approach challenges with a calm, objective view.	Mindfulness practices and self-reflection can help enhance clarity by allowing you to observe your thoughts without judgement.

Curiosity			
Curiosity reflects an open-minded interest in understanding oneself and others without judgement. It's an open-minded and accepting attitude toward your feelings, thoughts, and the behaviours of others.	When you are curious, you're genuinely interested in understanding what drives feelings like fears, desires, and motivations and the behaviours of others. You don't approach situations with preconceived notions or judgments, allowing you to be more empathetic and open to growth.	Curiosity can disarm defensive behaviours. Instead of reacting with frustration or avoidance, you ask yourself, "Why am I feeling this way?" or "What does this emotion need?" This leads to deeper self-awareness and healthier relationships.	Practise asking yourself compassionate questions when emotions arise. Stay open to learning more about yourself and others, even in moments of discomfort.

Compassion			
A deep sense of caring and empathy for oneself and others. Compassion is the ability to extend kindness and understanding toward yourself and others, especially when facing pain or difficulty.	When you operate from a calm space, you naturally feel compassionate toward distress. Compassion allows you to acknowledge suffering without judgement and to respond with care and support.	Compassionate self-leadership heals inner wounds, transforms self-criticism into self-love, and builds stronger, more compassionate relationships. When you are compassionate toward yourself, you are better able to offer that same care to others.	Practise self-compassion by speaking to yourself kindly in difficult moments and acknowledging your struggles without harsh judgement. Extend that same empathy to others, even when they're difficult to understand.

Confidence			
Trust in one's ability to handle life's challenges and lead effectively. Confidence comes from trusting in your own capacity to navigate life's challenges and to lead your emotional landscape with wisdom and care	Confidence is not arrogance or overestimating your abilities. It's a grounded belief in your resilience and strength, recognising that you can manage difficult emotions and situations. When you are confident, you don't feel the need to hide behind defensive or protective emotions.	Confidence allows you to take ownership of your life, make decisions with conviction, and engage with the world in an empowered way. You don't need to control or avoid emotions or the emotions of others because you trust that you can handle whatever comes.	Build confidence by acknowledging your strengths and past successes. Engage with challenges as opportunities for growth rather than as threats.

Courage			
The willingness to face difficult emotions, memories, or situations without fear getting in the way. Courage is the bravery to confront uncomfortable feelings, difficult memories, or challenging situations, even when it feels safer to avoid or ignore them.	Courage comes from the strength to hold space for your more vulnerable emotions. It's the willingness to explore parts of you that have been hidden, repressed, or exiled because they are painful to face.	Courage enables deep healing because it allows you to approach your pain and discomfort with acceptance rather than avoidance. When you have courage, you can create real change, both internally and in your external life.	Acknowledge your fears and then take small steps toward facing them. Courage grows with practice as you learn to handle discomfort and uncertainty.

Creativity			
The ability to find new, flexible ways to respond to challenges. Creativity is the capacity to think outside of habitual patterns and find new solutions to problems. It involves flexibility and openness to trying different approaches to old challenges.	Creativity means that you are not confined to rigid ways of thinking or behaving. Creativity allows you to engage with life from a place of playfulness and innovation, seeking novel ways to meet your needs and heal your wounds.	Creativity opens up possibilities where once there seemed to be none. It helps break through the stagnation of old patterns, allowing you to adapt and evolve in more fulfilling ways.	Embrace activities that spark your imagination, like art, writing, or music. When faced with a challenge, ask yourself, "What's a new way I could approach this?"

Connectedness			
A sense of connection with oneself and others, promoting relationships and belonging. Connectedness is the feeling of being deeply connected to yourself and the world around you. It's the awareness that you are part of something larger that encourages a sense of belonging and interdependence.	When you are connected, you can lead your internal landscape harmoniously and engage with others in meaningful, empathetic ways. Connectedness breaks down feelings of isolation and helps you build nurturing relationships, both within yourself and with others.	A sense of connectedness creates emotional safety, fostering vulnerability and authenticity in relationships. When you feel connected, you are better equipped to connect deeply with others, forming bonds based on mutual understanding and respect.	Engage in practices that create self-awareness and empathy, such as meditation, journaling, or spending time in nature. Build relationships that support authentic, compassionate communication.

Core Self Visualisation for developing the qualities of the 8 Cs

Preparation

- Find a quiet, serene space where you won't be disturbed.
- Sit or lie down comfortably, closing your eyes.
- Take a few deep, slow breaths, allowing your body to relax and your mind to quieten.

Visualising Your Sanctuary

Imagine yourself in a lush, verdant forest bathed in soft, dappled sunlight. The air is filled with the sweet scent of pine needles and the gentle rustle of leaves. A gentle breeze carries the distant melody of a babbling brook.

Feel the cool, moist earth beneath your feet, grounding you in the present moment. The towering trees, reaching for the sky, symbolise your connection to something greater than yourself.

Calling In the Core Qualities of Self

For these exercises, start by envisioning a radiant, golden light descending from above, enveloping you in its warm embrace. As this light touches you, feel a sense of peace and tranquillity wash over you.

- **Calmness**

Picture a serene lake, its surface as smooth as glass, reflecting the serene sky. The air is still, and the only sound is the gentle lapping of water against the shore.

Breathe deeply, inhaling the tranquillity of the scene. Feel your body relaxing, your mind calming, and your spirit finding its centre.

- **Clarity**

Imagine yourself standing on a mountaintop overlooking a vast, fog-free landscape. The air is crisp and clear, and the horizon stretches endlessly.

Take a deep breath, inhaling the purity of the air. Feel your mind becoming sharp and focused, free from confusion and doubt.

- **Curiosity**

Envision yourself wandering through a vibrant, exotic garden. A kaleidoscope of colours, textures, and scents fills the air. Each plant and flower is unique, inviting you to explore and discover.

Breathe in the spirit of curiosity. Feel your mind opening up to new ideas, perspectives, and experiences.

- **Compassion**

Place your hand on your heart and feel its gentle rhythm. Imagine a warm, golden light emanating from your heart, spreading love and kindness to all beings.

Breathe in the warmth of compassion. Feel your heart opening to empathy, understanding, and forgiveness.

- **Confidence**

Visualise yourself as a majestic oak tree rooted firmly in the ground. Your branches reach towards the sky, strong and unwavering.

Breathe in the strength and stability of the tree. Feel your confidence growing and your self-belief strengthening.

- **Courage**

Picture a fearless lion, his eyes bright and focused. It stands tall, ready to face any challenge with courage and determination.

Breathe in the courage of the lion. Feel your fear dissolving, replaced by a sense of bravery and resilience.

- **Creativity**

Imagine yourself standing in front of an empty canvas, watching the different coloured brush strokes move on the surface. Each stroke is unique, ever-changing, and full of potential.

Breathe in the creativity of the lines, colours, and textures. Feel your mind becoming more flexible, innovative, and imaginative.

- **Connectedness**

Envision yourself as part of a network. You feel a deep sense of belonging and connection to others.

Breathe in the warmth of connection. Feel your heart opening to love, friendship, and intimacy.

- **Concluding the Visualisation**

Take a few deep breaths, grounding yourself in the present moment. Bring yourself back to your present situation.

Slowly open your eyes, carrying, maintaining and treasuring the peace, clarity, and strength you've cultivated within with these exercises.

CHAPTER 10 - THE CARDINAL DIRECTIONS OF COMPASSIONATE RECOVERY: NAVIGATING THE STORM

FROM GRIDLOCK TO GROWTH

I'm trapped in bumper-to-bumper traffic, my grip tightening on the steering wheel as frustration mounts with each agonising inch forward. Every car feels like an immovable barrier, amplifying the slow crawl that seems endless. "These inconsiderate drivers!" I mutter under my breath, scanning for the cause of this maddening gridlock. There's no single culprit. It's the entire situation. I'm adrift in a sea of impatience, all of us contributing to the very problem we rage against. A loud honk pierces the air. It startles me and summons me back to this chaotic moment. The driver next to me is a mirror image of my own annoyance. Their anger is not directed at me specifically but at the situation we share.

A shock goes through me as I realise I'm not just a frustrated bystander surrounded by fools. I'm part of it, a single thread woven into the tangled web of annoyance that is this traffic jam. The blame I fling outward boomerang back, hitting me sharply in the chest. I take a deep breath and try to relax my tense shoulders. The traffic remains chaotic, but my perspective is changing. This isn't a battlefield, and I'm not a victim. I'm an observer, caught in the same muddle as everyone else.

Instead of judging the scene with a critical eye, I become curious and start observing. The world, previously obscured by frustration, moves into focus. The steady drone of the engine becomes a grounding force, a constant amid the chaos. Details once overlooked come into sharp focus: the intricate airbrushed designs on a passing truck, the determined gleam in the eyes of a cyclist weaving through traffic. My attention turns inward, anchoring me in the present. Frustration starts to fade, replaced not by resignation but by a quiet acceptance. I may not control the traffic, but I can control my response. As I release my judgement, a sense of calmness settles over me. This newfound skill is about accepting reality without judgement.

I inhale, relax my stiff shoulders and feel a wave of forgiveness wash over me. I forgive the impatient driver, forgive the seemingly endless traffic, and forgive myself for allowing the negativity to consume me. In its wake, a flicker of hope ignited within me. Maybe I could use this time productively by listening to a podcast, or maybe I could simply appreciate this unexpected moment of introspection and revelation. The traffic jam remained, but I was no longer a prisoner within it. I was a participant, enjoying the freedom of my newfound awareness, acceptance, agency, and a spark of hope illuminating the path forward.

My story illustrates the transformative power of non-judgement in a frustrating situation. Initially, I was fixated on external factors such as the slow traffic and inconsiderate drivers. These external factors fuelled the anger and blame I felt. Consequently, it resulted in a negative internal experience. However, a turning point came when I realised I was part of the "traffic", not separate from it. This shift in perspective fostered a sense of response-ability (the ability to respond rather than react) for my own experience. By letting go of blame, my focus naturally turned inward.

This inward shift allowed for greater awareness. Instead of dwelling on uncontrollable elements, I began observing the present moment. I became aware of the sights, sounds, and sensations of the environment. Mindful observation replaced frustration with acceptance of the situation as it was. Furthermore, my experience highlighted the unexpected benefits of taking responsibility for my own experience. Releasing blame opened the door to positive emotions such as acceptance, forgiveness, and hope. I forgave the impatient driver, the traffic, and even myself for getting caught up in negativity. This emotional shift paved the way for a spark of hope, a newfound sense of optimism that something positive might be found within the experience.

Relevance to Compassionate Recovery: A Non-Judgemental Approach

In the journey of compassionate recovery, we often encounter a complex landscape of cravings and negative emotions like anger, shame, and guilt. These internal experiences can be overwhelming and potentially derail progress. However, a non-judgemental approach, as illustrated in the story, can provide a valuable tool while facing these challenges. By observing cravings and emotions without criticism, you can develop a better understanding of your patterns and triggers. This non-judgemental stance allows for a more constructive response, preventing self-blame and shame that can hinder recovery. It's the same as recognising that traffic jams are a part of the journey rather than personal failures.

Just as you are responsible for your own driving, you are ultimately responsible for your journey. While support is essential, the success of recovery depends on personal choices and actions. Embracing setbacks, like traffic jams, without judgement enables a calmer, more hopeful perspective. It's about acknowledging that challenges are a natural part of the process and using them as opportunities for growth.

Releasing blame and judgement can lead to unexpected positive emotions that are crucial for staying motivated and maintaining a positive outlook. This non-judgemental approach encourages a sense of self-compassion and resilience. These are essential qualities to utilise on the path to recovery.

Tools for Transformation

- **Mindful Observation:** Instead of judging, simply notice the sights, sounds, and sensations around you. Focus on the present moment without getting caught up in thoughts or judgements.
- **Self-Awareness:** Recognise your internal state and the emotions influencing your reactions. Practice mindfulness to observe your thoughts and feelings without judgement.
- **Letting Go of Blame:** Take responsibility for your own experience and release any negativity directed outward. Focus on your own actions and choices.
- **Acceptance:** Acknowledge the situation as it is without judgement. Practice non-judgemental awareness to embrace the present moment, including its challenges.

Reflective Prompts

Reflection	Prompt	Your thoughts
Think of a recent situation that caused you frustration or anger.	How did you initially react?	

Identify any "traffic jams" in your own life (e.g., negative thought patterns, unhealthy habits).	➢ How do these patterns affect your well-being?	
Consider how practising mindful observation could help you navigate these situations differently.	➢ What might you notice about your thoughts and feelings if you simply observe them without judgement?	
Consider a situation where you're currently holding onto blame.	➢ How does holding onto blame affect you emotionally and physically? ➢ What might it feel like to release the blame?	
Imagine accepting a challenging situation without judgement.	➢ What emotions might surface? ➢ How might this acceptance affect your overall well-being?	

NAVIGATING THE STORM

Aerin, a name as vast and deep as the ocean she loved, felt the icy spray sting her eyes as a monstrous wave crashed against her sailboat. The sickening creak of the vessel resounded the hollowness she felt within her. Lost at sea, both literally and figuratively, she clutched the helm, her knuckles white with a grip that mirrored the storm's fury. Years of chasing mirages left her unfulfilled. The numbing escape of addiction had led her to this desolate place. She was lost without any hope or direction. Joy felt like a cruel joke, a distant delusion mocking her from the horizon. Despair, like a cold, suffocating wave, threatened to engulf her.

Suddenly, a flicker of defiance battled the storm's relentless assault. A bright light that illuminated the horizon appeared. Squinting through the torrential rain, she saw a beacon slicing through the oppressive darkness. It was a lighthouse, resolute and unwavering, its powerful beam sweeping across the tumultuous waves like a guiding hand in the chaos. Hope, a surge so powerful it defied the storm's roar, ran through her. She steered the battered boat towards it, the inscription on the lighthouse slowly coming into focus. With each agonising inch closer, the words blazed into clarity: "Elysian Beacon".

Aerin studied Greek mythology at school and knew that the name was derived from the Elysian Fields, which represented a paradise of perfect happiness. It symbolised hope, solace, and a journey toward inner tranquillity and fulfilment. Cast in radiant light, the inscription stood as a promise and a beacon of salvation etched against the storm's fury. It was a pathway of solace and redemption, a guiding light leading her out of the tempest and into the embrace of safety and healing. Exhausted, Aerin stumbled onto a windswept shore, the world spinning as the fury of the sea continued its unsettling assault. A vertical shaft of golden light beckoned her. Dragging herself toward it, a half-opened door came into view.

Aerin entered hesitantly, giving her eyes time to adjust to the light. Before her stood a woman, her weathered face a canvas of time. Deep lines spoke of countless adventures and hard-earned wisdom. "Welcome, wanderer," the woman's voice, gentle against the storm's resounding turmoil, soothed Aerin's ragged breaths. "Many souls have been battered by these tides, searching for solace on fleeting shores," the woman said, placing her hand over her heart. "Not knowing that what they seek already resides within. The compass toward authenticity, inner peace, and a meaningful life lies not outside you but within."

For some strange reason, the woman's words resonated deeply with Aerin. Instead of a map, she offered a compass, its worn surface inscribed with four guiding principles for conquering tumultuous seas. The woman's words struck a deep chord in Aerin. Rather than a map, she offered a compass pendant - its weathered surface etched with four letters, each hinting at a guiding principle for navigating stormy seas.

Aerin glanced at the letter R on her pendant; the first cardinal direction termed **Response-ability**. This, she was told, was about navigating life more effectively. By becoming response-able, Aerin could acknowledge her authority and the power to steer a different course.

The second direction was **Acceptance**. The storm wouldn't vanish overnight. Acceptance meant acknowledging the churning waves and the fear gripping her heart. This referred to the acceptance of the reality of the situation. It was the foundation upon which she could build resilience and healthy coping strategies.

Forgiveness followed as a direction. Shame, anger, and resentment were heavy weights dragging her down. Once Aerin accepted reality, she could start to forgive. Forgiveness didn't mean condoning her actions or others' but releasing the chains that bound her. It was the key to moving forward.

The final direction was **Hope**. Despite the storm's fury, there was always a sliver of hope, determination, a guiding star on the darkest and stormiest nights.

Emboldened by a rekindled fire within, Aerin faced the churning sea once more. The storm roared like a relentless beast, but a defiant determination burned in Aerin's eyes. With each crashing wave, she clung to the compass's instructions:

- Take responsibility
- Embrace reality
- Extend forgiveness
- Embrace hope

The journey ahead had its challenges, but Aerin was no longer adrift and hopeless. The compass with the four cardinal directions (Response-ability, Acceptance, Forgiveness, Hope) guided her towards a newfound sense of peace and purpose.

THE 4 CARDINAL DIRECTIONS: PLANNING YOUR RECOVERY JOURNEY

The 4 Cardinal Directions is a comprehensive framework designed to guide you through your recovery journey, much like a compass helps a sailor navigate stormy seas.

Just as the four cardinal directions (north, south, east, and west) provide a navigational framework on a map, these guiding principles (Response-ability, Acceptance, Forgiveness, and Hope) serve as internal compass points to help you face life's challenges. By incorporating these principles in your life, you can develop a deeper understanding of yourself, your experiences, and your path to recovery.

The 1st Cardinal Direction – Response-Ability: The Foundation of Empowerment

This direction represents the ability to take control of how you respond to life's challenges. By embracing response-ability, you stop attributing blame to external circumstances and instead focus on how you can actively shape your outcomes. This empowers you to see obstacles not as roadblocks but as opportunities for growth and learning.

- **Response:** According to the Oxford Dictionary, "response" means "a reaction to something". It implies a thoughtful and considered reaction rather than an impulsive one.
- **Ability:** The Oxford Dictionary defines "ability" as "the power or capacity to do something". In this context, it refers to the capability to respond in a particular way.

In the context of compassionate recovery, "response-ability" means the ability to respond to life's challenges and situations in a mindful, compassionate, and intentional way. It involves:

- **Self-awareness:** Understanding your thoughts, feelings, and triggers.

- **Mindfulness:** Being present in the moment and observing your thoughts and emotions without judgment.
- **Compassion:** Treating yourself and others with kindness, understanding, and forgiveness.
- **Intentionality:** Making conscious choices about how you respond to situations.

Key Implications of Response-ability

- **Empowerment:** By taking responsibility for your responses, you gain control over your life and your recovery.
- **Healing:** Compassionate responses promote emotional healing and well-being.
- **Healthy Relationships:** Response-ability promotes healthier relationships with yourself and others.
- **Resilience:** The ability to respond mindfully helps you build resilience and cope with challenges.

The concept of **Response-ability** encourages you to shift your focus inward. While external events undoubtedly play a role in your life, substantial research suggests that your thoughts and behaviours have a significant influence on your well-being. Response-ability empowers you to take ownership of your responses and cultivate a more sustainable sense of well-being grounded in your internal world and your ability to choose how you react to life's challenges.

By embracing Response-ability, you acknowledge that while you cannot control every event that happens to you, you have the power to control your responses and attitudes. This perspective shift transforms your approach to well-being from a passive search for external sources of happiness or despair to an active engagement with your internal processes.

The Power of Response-Ability: Viktor Frankl's Legacy

Viktor Frankl, a Holocaust survivor and renowned psychiatrist, offered a profound insight into human resilience:

"Between stimulus and response, there is a space. In that space lies our power to choose our response. In our response lies our growth and our freedom."

Frankl's experiences in a concentration camp inspired him to develop logotherapy, a theory that emphasises the importance of finding meaning in life, even in the most challenging circumstances. Response-ability is often misunderstood as simply accepting blame for outcomes. However, it is about recognising the space between external events and our internal reactions. It is the power to become the author of our own experiences rather than passive victims of circumstances. By choosing our responses mindfully, we can shape our lives, encourage resilience, and discover meaning even in the face of adversity.

Mindful Reflection Tool: Tapping into Your Inner Wisdom

STEP 1: **Identify a Challenge**	Choose a current challenge you're facing. This could be a personal, professional, or interpersonal issue.
Step 2: **Create a Sacred Space**	Find a quiet, comfortable place where you won't be disturbed.
Step 3: **Mindful Presence**	Sit comfortably and focus on your breath. Notice the sensations you feel and the sounds around you.
Step 4: **Connect with Your Inner Wisdom**	Imagine your Wise Mind (DBT), Self (IFS), or Wise Elder sitting beside you. This could be a personified version of your inner wisdom, intuition, or higher self.
Step 5: **Pose Your Question**	Ask your inner guide, "How can I best address this challenge?" or "What wisdom can you offer me to help me through this?"
Step 6: **Listen and Record**	Pay attention to the thoughts, feelings, and insights that arise. Write down everything that comes to mind, even if it seems random or nonsensical.

Example:

- **Challenge:** Feeling overwhelmed by work deadlines and personal responsibilities.
- **Inner Guide:** "Remember your priorities. Focus on the most important tasks first. Don't be afraid to delegate or ask for help. Take breaks and practice self-care to avoid burnout."

Tips:

- **Be patient:** Allow your inner wisdom time to emerge.
- **Trust your intuition:** Even if the insights seem unusual, trust that they are coming from a deeper part of yourself.
- **Reflect on your responses:** After the exercise, carefully consider the insights you received. Think about how you can apply them to your challenges.

By tapping into your inner wisdom through this mindful reflection tool, you can gain valuable insights, reduce stress, and find creative solutions to your challenges.

The Duality Within: A Cherokee Tale

Imagine a Cherokee village and an elder renowned for his wisdom gathering the villagers around a crackling fire. As the dancing flames cast shadows, he tells a tale of two wolves residing within each of us. One wolf, cloaked in dark shadows, embodies fear, unhealthy anger, blame, resentment, and shame. The other, bathed in sunlight, represents responsibility, acceptance, compassion, and forgiveness. The elder doesn't tell the villagers which wolf will grow but poses a powerful question: "Which wolf will you choose to feed?"

The tale invites you to contemplate the internal struggle between these two opposing forces within yourself. It suggests that your choices and actions determine which wolf ultimately prevails. By nurturing the wolf of responsibility, acceptance, compassion, and forgiveness, you can promote a more positive and fulfilling life.

Reclaiming your Narrative: Beyond Passive Acceptance

Life is a constant dialogue. From the moment you enter the world, you receive messages that influence your journey. However, you are not a passive recipient. You have the power to interpret and respond to these messages, shaping your reality. Response-ability, then, isn't about passively enduring events but becoming the author of your experiences. Response-ability requires courage. It asks you to delve into your emotional landscape, understand your vulnerabilities, and view experiences as opportunities for growth. You can choose to succumb to negativity and blame or embrace the power of a constructive response.

As Ramana Maharshi, the Indian sage, said, "If your feet hurt, there are two things you can do – you can wrap the whole world in burlap, or you can buy a pair of shoes." Choose the shoes. Take ownership and embrace response-ability. Walk with purpose and forge a path of healing, empowerment, and liberation.

Resources

Theme	Title	Author
Mindfulness-Based Stress Reduction (MBSR)	***Mindfulness: A Practical Guide to Finding Peace in a Frantic World***	Jon Kabat-Zinn
Dialectical Behaviour Therapy (DBT)	***The Dialectical Behavior Therapy Skills Workbook: Practical Exercises to Help You Live a Full and Balanced Life***	Marsha M. Linehan

Acceptance and Commitment Therapy (ACT)	***The Happiness Trap: How to Stop Struggling and Start Living***	Russ Harris
Compassionate Inquiry	***Compassionate Inquiry: A Journey of Self-Discovery and Healing***	Tara Brach
	Internal Family Systems Therapy	Richard Schwartz and Martha Sweezy
Internal Family Systems (IFS)	***No Bad Parts: Healing Trauma and Restoring Wholeness with the Internal Family Systems Model***	Richard Schwartz
	Self-Therapy: A Step-by-Step Guide to Creating Inner Wholeness Using IFS	Jay Earley
Trauma-Informed Therapy	***The Body Keeps the Score: Brain, Mind, and Body in the Healing of Trauma***	Bessel van der Kolk

The 2nd Cardinal Direction – Acceptance: The Path to Understanding

Acceptance serves as the grounding force in your journey. It involves acknowledging your reality without resistance. This creates a stable foundation for healing. Acceptance doesn't mean resignation but rather recognising the truth of your situation so that you can move forward with clarity and peace. In active addiction, you might find yourself locked in a relentless battle with your painful emotions and destructive habits. You identify these as unwelcome aspects of yourself that you desperately try to avoid or eradicate. You may deny, suppress, hide, or attempt to fix them, often resorting to self-criticism and condemnation. However, this internal war is typically a losing battle.

The Power of Complete Surrender: Shadow Work and Your Inner Critic

- **Shadow Work**: This practice helps uncover and integrate the hidden parts of yourself – traits, emotions, or memories you reject or suppress – leading to greater self-awareness and healing.
- **The Inner Critic**: By understanding and transforming the internal voice of self-judgement, you can develop a kinder, more supportive relationship with yourself.

Shadow Work: Embracing the Parts of Yourself You've Rejected

What is Shadow Work?

Shadow work is the process of exploring and integrating the parts of yourself that you've suppressed, ignored, or rejected. This is what psychologist Carl Jung called the "shadow." These hidden aspects often hold emotions, traits, or memories that you deem "unacceptable" due to societal expectations, family dynamics, or personal experiences. Left unacknowledged, the shadow can influence your life in unconscious ways, creating patterns of fear, shame, self-sabotage, or unfulfilled potential.

Mindfulness and Acceptance in Shadow Work

The key to shadow work lies in acceptance. Instead of pushing uncomfortable thoughts and feelings away, mindfulness allows us to approach your shadow with curiosity, compassion, and non-judgement. When you stop resisting what you fear or dislike, you create space to understand and integrate these aspects, leading to greater wholeness and inner peace.

How to Practice Shadow Work with Acceptance

1. **Recognise Your Shadow Triggers**

- Notice moments when you feel strong emotional reactions – anger, jealousy, shame, or insecurity. These reactions often point to parts of your shadow that want to be seen.
- Practice: Pause, take a deep breath, and ask, "What am I feeling right now? Why does this trigger me?"

2. Journal with Compassion

Write about the traits, emotions, or memories you suppress or deny. Approach this process without judgement.

Prompt: "What qualities or behaviours in others irritate me, and could this reflect something in myself?"

Accept that these traits don't make you "bad" – they are part of your human experience.

3. Dialogue with Your Shadow

- Visualise your shadow as a younger or vulnerable version of yourself. Sit with this version and ask:
- "What do you need from me?"
- "How have you been trying to protect me?"
- Respond with kindness, acknowledging the purpose your shadow once served, even if it's no longer helpful.

4. Practice Self-Acceptance

- Use mindfulness to notice thoughts of self-judgement when exploring your shadow. Instead of resisting, observe and accept them.
- Mantra: "All parts of me are welcome. I accept myself fully, even the parts I do not yet understand."

Why Shadow Work Matters

Shadow work allows us to:

- **Break Free from Patterns:** Unconscious behaviours driven by the shadow lose power when brought into awareness.
- **Find Hidden Gifts:** Repressed traits like assertiveness, creativity, or sensitivity can be reclaimed and celebrated.
- **Heal Inner Wounds:** By accepting and integrating your shadow, you reduce shame and foster self-compassion.
- When you stop running from the darkness within, you discover that it holds the light of transformation.

Your Inner Critic: Transforming Judgement into Acceptance

What is the Inner Critic?

The inner critic is the internal voice of self-judgement that often berates you for not being "good enough", "successful enough", or "perfect". It arises from societal conditioning, past experiences, and a desire to avoid failure or rejection. While the critic may mean to protect you, its harshness can stifle confidence, creativity, and self-compassion.

Acceptance: The Key to Befriending the Inner Critic

Mindfulness teaches you to observe the inner critic with curiosity and acceptance rather than resistance or shame. Instead of believing or fighting its harsh words, you can learn to understand its origins and respond with compassion. By doing so, you transform this voice from an adversary into an ally.

Practices to Work with Your Inner Critic

1. **Notice and Name the Voice**

- Pay attention to when the inner critic appears. Give it a name or identity (e.g., "Critical Carl" or "Perfectionist Patty") to externalise it and reduce its power.

- Practice: Say to yourself, "Ah, there's my critic again. I see you, but I don't have to listen to you."

2. Observe Without Judgement

Mindfulness allows you to observe the inner critic without engaging with its negativity.

- Practice: When critical thoughts arise, pause and notice them as mental events, not facts.
- Repeat: "These are just thoughts. I don't have to believe them."

3. Dialogue with Compassion

- Once you've recognised the inner critic, respond with a kinder, more supportive voice.
  Ask: "What is the critic trying to protect me from? What does it fear?"

- Replace harsh words with acceptance:
  Critic: "You're going to fail."
  You: "It's okay to fail. I'm learning, and that's enough."

4. Write a Compassionate Letter to Yourself

- Imagine you're comforting a dear friend who feels inadequate or ashamed. Write a letter to yourself using that same empathy and care.
- Affirm: "I am enough as I am. Mistakes are part of growth. I don't have to be perfect to be worthy."

Why Working with the Inner Critic Matters

Transforming the inner critic leads to:

- **Greater Self-Acceptance:** You stop defining yourself by mistakes or imperfections.
- **Increased Confidence:** When freed from harsh judgement, you take more creative and courageous steps.
- **Emotional Resilience:** You learn to offer yourself compassion during challenges rather than falling into self-blame.
- When you accept the inner critic instead of fighting it, you reclaim your power. You realise that this voice does not define you – it is simply one part of your story.

Facing and Embracing Your Demons

The word "demon" comes from the ancient Greek term "daimōn" (δαίμων), which originally referred to a neutral or even positive supernatural being that served as an intermediary between gods and humans. Unlike the modern association with evil, daimōns were seen as divine forces or guides that influenced human lives, offering inspiration, protection, or wisdom. They embodied both light and shadow aspects of existence, sometimes sparking creativity and growth while at other times presenting challenges or disruptions that guided people toward greater self-awareness and transformation.

If this story feels triggering or uncomfortable, I invite you to explore alternative practices that serve a similar purpose:

After years of seclusion in his mountain retreat, Milarepa, a twelfth-century Tibetan master, returned to his cave to find it filled with demons. Despite understanding they were mere projections of his own mind, their presence was no less terrifying. Desperate to rid himself of these manifestations, he first tried to teach them spiritual truths, hoping they would disappear. They ignored him. Frustrated and angry, he charged at them, attempting to force them out. The demons, far stronger than him, only laughed.

Exhausted and defeated, Milarepa finally surrendered. He sat down and said, "I'm not leaving, and it seems you aren't either. So let's just live here together."

To his surprise, the moment he stopped resisting, most of the demons got up and left the cave. Only one remained as a particularly powerful and menacing presence. Realising that his only option was to deepen his surrender, Milarepa approached the demon, placed his head inside its enormous mouth, and said, "If you want to eat me, go ahead."

In that moment, the demon vanished. Through this experience, Milarepa discovered a poignant truth: true freedom comes when we stop resisting entirely and let go of judgement, control, tension, and avoidance. In this open, tender acceptance, there is no place for painful shadow energies to take root.

With the surrender of all self-protective strategies, the demons lose their power. When the resistance disappears, so do the demons.

Mindfulness emphasises acceptance as recognising and embracing the present moment without judgement or resistance. It involves acknowledging your thoughts, feelings, and sensations as they are rather than wishing for them to be different. Acceptance isn't passive – it encourages peace with reality, enabling more effective responses to situations. By cultivating acceptance, you pave the way for personal growth, emotional balance, and deeper self-understanding. It helps break the cycle of suffering linked to resisting reality, allowing for clearer, more compassionate and resilient reactions to challenges.

Mindfulness Tool: The Power of Complete Surrender

Instructions

- **Identify a Challenging Situation:** Think about a situation that is currently causing you stress or discomfort.
- **Mindful Observation:** Observe your thoughts, feelings, and sensations related to this situation. Notice any judgements, criticisms, or desires to change the situation.
- **Practice Surrender:** Imagine yourself sitting in a cave, surrounded by the demons of your inner turmoil. Instead of fighting them, try to accept their presence.

- **Let Go of Resistance:** Surrender your desire to control the situation, change your feelings, or avoid discomfort. Focus on simply being present with the experience.
- **Embrace the Moment:** Allow yourself to feel the emotions without judgement or resistance. Observe the thoughts and sensations that arise.
- **Notice the Shift:** As you practise surrender, observe any changes in your experience. Does your darkness or the shadows of your inner turmoil lose their power over you? Do you feel a sense of peace or acceptance?

Dialectical Behaviour Therapy Tool: Willingness

Willingness is a core skill in DBT that involves accepting the present moment without judgement or resistance. It's about being open to whatever arises, even if it's uncomfortable or painful.

How to Practice Willingness

- **Identify Resistance:** Notice when you're resisting the present moment. This might involve thoughts like "I shouldn't be feeling this way" or "I wish things were different."
- **Accept the Present Moment:** Remind yourself that the present moment is all there is. Avoid dwelling on the past or worrying about the future.
- **Practice Mindfulness:** Focus on your breath or sensations in your body to stay present.
- **Focus on Your Values:** Remember what is important to you and how accepting the present moment can help you move towards your goals.

Radical Acceptance: Embracing the Full Story

Radical acceptance encourages you to fully embrace reality, including its messy and uncomfortable aspects. It is not about naive optimism – instead, it involves acknowledging the complete picture with all its imperfections and finding peace within that understanding.

Letting Go of Resistance

We often fight against discomfort, clinging to a fantasy of how things "should be." Radical acceptance encourages us to release this futile struggle. Picture gripping a doorknob tightly instead of simply turning it – that's the resistance we create by fighting against reality, which only intensifies our suffering. In contrast, radical acceptance invites us to find peace with what is, even when it feels uncomfortable.

Tara Brach, a renowned teacher of radical acceptance, offers valuable insights

- **Ditching the "Not Enough" Story:** We often chase an illusion of perfection, leading to a constant feeling of inadequacy. Radical acceptance helps us see our inherent worth exactly as we are in this moment.
- **The Power of Self-Compassion:** Treating ourselves with kindness like we would a cherished friend encourages inner peace and resilience.
- **Befriending Your Emotions:** All emotions hold value. Radical acceptance encourages us to understand and accept our emotions, even the negative ones. There's wisdom to be learned from anger, sadness, or fear.
- **Surrendering to What Is:** We waste a lot of energy trying to control the uncontrollable. Radical acceptance enables us to release this struggle and embrace a more liberated way of living.
- **Mindfulness as a Guide:** By being fully present in the moment, we free ourselves from dwelling on the past or worrying about the future. This awareness promotes a sense of inner calm.
- **Deeper Connections:** When we accept ourselves fully, warts and all,

we open ourselves to deeper, more authentic connections with others. This self-acceptance allows us to embrace others' imperfections, paving the way for genuine relationships rooted in mutual understanding.

TOOLS FOR ACCEPTANCE AND RADICAL ACCEPTANCE

Acceptance

- **Journaling:** Write about your experiences and emotions surrounding your situation. Acknowledge what is happening without judgement.
- **Gratitude Practice:** Focus on the things you are grateful for, even amidst challenges. This can help shift your perspective and create acceptance.
- **Mindfulness Meditation:** Focus on the present moment and observe your thoughts and feelings without judgement. This can help you detach from negativity and accept what is.
- **Identify Your Needs:** Reflect on your basic needs and how your current situation might be affecting them. Focus on fulfilling those needs in healthy ways.
- **Letting Go Exercises:** Visualise yourself releasing negative emotions or the need to control the situation.

Radical Acceptance

- **The "Willingness Statement":** Create a statement like "I am willing to accept that..." followed by the aspect of your situation you're struggling with. Repeat it regularly as a mantra.
- **The "What Is" Exercise:** When difficult emotions arise, acknowledge them and say, "This is what is happening right now." This simple act can anchor you in the present and reduce resistance.
- **Loving-Kindness Meditation:** Practice sending yourself loving thoughts and affirmations. This cultivates self-compassion, a key element of radical acceptance.

- **Radical Acceptance of Emotions:** Allow yourself to feel all your emotions, even the uncomfortable ones. Observe them without judgement and see them as temporary states.
- **Focus on What You Can Control:** Identify the aspects of your situation that you can influence and focus your energy there.
- **Radical Acceptance of Imperfections:** Recognise that you and your situation will never be perfect. Embrace the beauty of growth, progress and imperfection.

The 3rd Cardinal Direction – Forgiveness: The Key to Healing

Forgiveness clears your path by letting go of past grievances. It's like a gentle wind that disperses the fog of resentment, allowing you to see more clearly. Forgiving others and yourself releases the burdens of anger and bitterness, freeing you to build deeper, meaningful connections.

Finding Relief from Resentment and Blame

Sean felt a deep anger rising within him, a mix of bitterness and disappointment that had built up over the years. He carried a heavy sense of shame, which weighed down on him. Years of self-blame and regret clouded his life. Everything felt empty and devoid of joy. His heart felt desolate, filled only with sharp reminders of his pain and grief.

Then, in the supportive environment of a recovery group, a small light began to emerge. Surrounded by people who shared similar struggles, he heard voices of encouragement and understanding. A supportive word from a fellow member, the shared stories of resilience, and moments of collective empathy acted like lifelines in lifting his spirits. With each meeting, he began to feel a sense of belonging and connection. Slowly, the tightness in his chest started to ease.

The walls he had built from shame and disappointment started to weaken. He felt an urge to break free. In his search for peace, Sean turned to meditation, discovering new techniques to calm his mind. During these moments of mindfulness, he pictured a seed. This once-hardened shell of anger began to soften, opening up to the possibility of growth. Sunlight poured through the cracks, revealing a tiny sprout, a symbol of hope emerging from within. His anger had transformed, no longer a burden but a catalyst for personal development. The tight shell of resentment surrendered to the warmth of light. The delicate sprout represented a journey toward healing and acceptance.

As the seed of change took root, Sean found strength in challenges, nurtured by the understanding and support of his recovery community. Self-compassion and forgiveness became the sunlight that helped him grow. Acknowledging his past and taking responsibility for his emotions allowed him to regain a sense of control over his life. Acceptance paved the way for healing.

The journey toward forgiveness and hope proved rewarding. As the seeds of change flourished, Sean uncovered resilience within himself. Forgiveness didn't mean forgetting or excusing the past; it was about releasing the emotional weight that came with it. In this process, he found renewed hope and the understanding that, even in difficult times, a glimmer of light is always within reach.

Self-Compassion: A Foundation for Forgiveness

Forgiveness cannot truly flourish without the nurturing soil of self-compassion. When you treat yourself with kindness and understanding, you create an environment conducive to the growth of forgiveness. Self-compassion allows you to heal internally, empathise with others, and break free from the destructive cycle of self-blame. By cultivating self-compassion, you can let go of anger and resentment, creating a gentler space for forgiveness to take root. You acknowledge that everyone makes mistakes, including yourself. This acknowledgement encourages empathy for those who have hurt you. This understanding bridges the gap between yourself and others, paving the way for forgiveness.

Furthermore, self-compassion helps you move beyond self-blame, a cycle that hinders forgiveness. You recognise that suffering is a natural part of life, not a reflection of your worthiness. This shift in perspective allows you to break free from the self-critical mindset that can impede your ability to forgive. Moreover, self-compassion acts as a buffer against harsh self-judgement, enabling you to bounce back from setbacks and continue on the path to forgiveness. When you treat yourself with kindness, you build resilience and create a stronger foundation for personal growth.

Finally, forgiveness rooted in self-compassion is genuine and long-lasting. It arises from a desire for healing rather than from external pressures. This desire for healing leads to deeper and more meaningful forgiveness. By cultivating self-compassion, you can embark on a journey of forgiveness that is truly transformative and liberating.

Forgiveness is a Part of the Healing Process

Forgiveness is often portrayed as a single, monumental act. However, the reality is far more nuanced. It's a journey, a series of steps that lead to healing. Let's explore the key stages of this path:

- **Acknowledgement:** The first critical step is acknowledgement. Confront the pain, whether caused by your actions or those of others. Name it, feel it, and allow yourself to grieve the loss or betrayal.

- **Examination:** Reflect on the impact of the hurt. How has it affected you and others? Understanding the depth of the wound is essential for complete healing.
- **Letting Go:** Clinging to anger, bitterness, and shame is like carrying a heavy weight. Forgiveness is the act of releasing the negative energy that consumes you. It's a conscious decision to let go of the emotional poison that binds you to the past.
- **Empathy:** Stepping into the other person's shoes, even if challenging, can cultivate compassion. Understanding their motives, limitations, or experiences doesn't excuse their behaviour but offers a broader perspective.
- **Forgiveness:** If appropriate and safe, consider offering a sincere apology and taking responsibility for your actions. This can pave the way for reconciliation and rebuilding trust. However, remember this step may not always be possible, especially in cases of abuse.
- **Boundaries:** Forgiveness doesn't mean vulnerability. Set healthy boundaries with yourself and others. Evaluate whether the relationship requires distance or even complete separation for you to move forward.
- **Self-Compassion:** Be kind to yourself throughout this process. Forgiveness can be a battle, and there will be setbacks. Practice self-compassion, acknowledging your struggles and celebrating your progress.
- **Support:** You don't have to walk this path alone. Lean on trusted friends, family members, a life coach, or a therapist. Sharing your journey can bring validation and empower you to move forward.
- **Patience:** Forgiveness isn't an overnight achievement. Be patient with yourself. It may take time to process the hurt, cultivate empathy, and release the negativity.
- **Transformation:** Ultimately, forgiveness is a gift you give yourself. It's an opportunity for personal growth and transformation. By letting go, you free yourself from the past and build a more resilient and compassionate future.

Ho'oponopono: A Path to Reconciliation and Forgiveness

Deeply rooted in Hawaiian culture and spirituality, Ho'oponopono was traditionally facilitated by respected elders or spiritual leaders. They guided communities in resolving conflicts, healing relationships, and restoring harmony.

Ho'oponopono is a powerful practice that offers a path towards reconciliation and forgiveness. It is a process of restoring balance and harmony within ourselves, with others, and with the divine. Imagine it as a tool to mend broken connections and cultivate inner peace.

Key Principles of Ho'oponopono:

- Self-Responsibility: Taking responsibility for your thoughts, feelings, and experiences.
- Forgiveness: Releasing negative emotions and forgiving yourself and others.
- Positive Affirmations: Repeating positive affirmations to cleanse your mind and heart.
- Divine Connection: Acknowledging your connection to a higher power or universal energy.

The Five Pillars of Ho'oponopono

1. **Taking Responsibility:** You acknowledge your role in creating disharmony, taking ownership of your thoughts, words, and actions.
2. **Repentance:** You sincerely apologise for any harm caused, acknowledging your mistakes and offering genuine remorse.
3. **Forgiveness:** You release resentment, anger, and negativity by forgiving yourself and others. Forgiveness is a gift you offer yourself, allowing you to move forward without burden.
4. **Gratitude:** You cultivate appreciation for the lessons learnt from experiences, both positive and negative. Gratitude encourages growth and helps you see the silver lining.

5. **Love and Compassion:** You nurture love and compassion for yourself and others, fostering understanding and empathy. This love extends to the situation itself, promoting healing.

The Power of Words: The Ho'oponopono Mantra

Ho'oponopono utilises a powerful mantra for internal reflection and transformation. Each phrase holds a unique meaning:

- "I'm Sorry": An acknowledgement of your contribution to negativity, a first step towards taking responsibility.
- "Please Forgive Me": Seeking forgiveness, not just from others but also from yourself. It's about releasing burdens and embracing self-compassion.
- "Thank You": Expressing gratitude for the opportunity to learn and grow, acknowledging the lessons hidden within each experience.
- "I Love You": A powerful affirmation of love for yourself, others involved, and the situation as a whole. Love is the driving force for healing and creating positive change.

Practicing Ho'oponopono

While traditionally practised in groups, Ho'oponopono can be incorporated into your daily life through meditation, prayer, or simply taking time for self-reflection. By repeating the mantra and reflecting on these principles, you can cultivate inner peace and build stronger, more harmonious relationships.

Ho'oponopono in Compassionate Recovery

Ho'oponopono can be a powerful tool in CR. Here's how you can incorporate it into your recovery journey:

Daily Practice:

- **Morning Mantra:** Begin your day by repeating the Ho'oponopono mantra: "I'm sorry. Please forgive me. Thank you. I love you."

- **Mindful Meditation:** Combine Ho'oponopono with mindfulness meditation. Focus on your breath while repeating the mantra, allowing yourself to become present with your thoughts and emotions.
- **Journaling:** Write about your experiences, feelings, and any insights that arise from your Ho'oponopono practice. This can help you to process emotions and identify patterns.

Relationship Building:

- **Interpersonal Forgiveness:** Use Ho'oponopono to address conflicts or resentments in your relationships. Practice forgiveness for yourself and others, even if you don't feel ready to reconcile.
- **Empathy and Understanding:** Promotes empathy for yourself and others. Remember that everyone is doing the best they can with the information and resources they have.
- **Compassionate Communication:** Use Ho'oponopono to approach conversations with compassion and understanding. Avoid blaming or shaming, and focus on finding common ground.

Self-Care:

- **Self-Compassion:** Treat yourself with kindness and understanding. Remember that you are doing your best and that it's okay to make mistakes.
- **Gratitude Practice:** Focus on the positive aspects of your life, no matter how small. Gratitude can help to shift your perspective and reduce stress.
- **Self-Forgiveness:** Release self-judgement and guilt. Practice forgiveness for your past mistakes and choices.

Healing and Growth:

- **Emotional Release:** Allow yourself to feel your emotions without judgement. Ho'oponopono can help you to process and release negative emotions.

- **Spiritual Connection:** Explore your spiritual beliefs and practices. Ho'oponopono can be a way to connect with a higher power or a sense of meaning.
- **Personal Growth:** Use Ho'oponopono as a tool for personal growth and transformation. Focus on becoming a better version of yourself.

Resource on Forgiveness

Flexible mind has heart: https://youtu.be/nq2OsN9ysgw?si=LhQxk9zFrobnU-FOP

The 4th Cardinal Direction Hope – The Beacon Illuminating the Path

Hope is not merely a wish for a better future – it is a conscious choice to live in the present moment and recognise that every decision you make brings you closer to or further from the life you desire. Hope is the guiding light that illuminates your path, even in the darkest times. It represents your belief in the possibility of positive change and gives you the courage to keep moving forward, no matter how difficult the journey may seem. With hope, you can manage life's challenges with a sense of purpose.

As Nick Cave once said, "Hopefulness is not a neutral position – it is adversarial. It is the warrior emotion that can lay waste to cynicism." In the journey of Compassionate Recovery, hopefulness becomes an act of defiance against despair. Often, hope is perceived as fragile, like a butterfly's wing. Yet it is a resilient warrior, forged through adversity and fuelled by the human spirit.

Hope is not blind optimism – it is a force driven by a belief in the possibility of positive change. It ignites courage and resilience, reminding us that even in the darkest storms, there is a way forward. True hope is a balanced perspective, acknowledging challenges while embracing the possibility of overcoming them. This foresight is essential, serving as a compass through the darkness toward transformation.

In recovery, hope acts as a catalyst, unlocking acceptance and forgiveness. By nurturing belief in change, hope helps you break free from resentment, paving the way for growth and trust. It empowers you to shed the victim mentality and embrace self-compassion. Hope is not wishful thinking about the future – it is grounded in present-moment awareness. It's about recognising the possibilities that exist within the present and believing in your ability to shape your own destiny. By focusing on the present moment, you can cultivate a sense of agency and empowerment, which are essential for fostering hope. It's about recognising the small steps you can take today to move towards your goals, even when the future may seem uncertain.

When Hope Becomes a Problem in Recovery

While hope can be a powerful force in recovery, it can also become problematic if it's overly focused on the future, preventing you from fully living in the present moment. If you wake up each morning solely focused on getting through the day until work is over, you're missing out on countless opportunities for joy and fulfilment. Similarly, if you keep postponing your life until that vacation or other special event, you may be neglecting the beauty and richness of the present moment.

Life is not about waiting for something better to happen. It's about finding joy in the little things, appreciating the present, and embracing the journey. We often think we can't be happy until we achieve a certain goal or attain a particular status. However, the truth is that life with a good relationship, more money, or a degree is still just life. True happiness and fulfilment come from living in the present moment and appreciating the beauty and richness of life as it is. By focusing on the here and now, you can cultivate a sense of peace, gratitude, and joy that will enrich your recovery journey.

Hope: A Beacon in the Storm of Life

Viktor Frankl, a Holocaust survivor and psychiatrist, significantly influenced our understanding of hope. His logotherapy and personal experiences emphasise the power of hope as a deep-seated belief in life's meaning, even amidst suffering. Frankl linked hope to finding meaning through suffering. In Man's Search for Meaning, he recounts his experiences and lessons. He observed that those finding meaning were more likely to survive. Hope, for Frankl, wasn't abstract but a practical force that emerged in his search for meaning. Central to Frankl's philosophy is the freedom to choose one's attitude toward circumstances. This includes choosing hope despite adversity. While you can't control external situations, you can decide how you respond. Choosing hope and meaning reinforces the indomitable nature of the human spirit.

Frankl's insights highlight hope's role as a catalyst for resilience and transformation. It enables you to transcend suffering by focusing on a larger purpose. This aligns with his broader view that the human spirit is inherently resilient and that you are capable of finding strength and meaning even in the darkest of times. Hope combats despair and fuels the quest for a fulfilling and purposeful life. Viktor Frankl's view on hope is a testament to its profound significance. It's not merely a passive feeling but an active, dynamic force that emerges from the search for meaning and purpose. By choosing hope and embracing a sense of purpose, you can navigate life's challenges, find resilience in suffering, and ultimately transform adversity into a source of strength and growth. Frankl's insights remind us that hope, deeply rooted in our human capacity for meaning, guides us through the storm towards a brighter, more purposeful future.

In Compassionate Recovery, this understanding of hope as a vital component in the journey of healing and transformation aligns with Frankl's philosophy of finding meaning and purpose through adversity. This approach helps you to harness hope as a powerful tool for overcoming challenges and achieving lasting recovery.

How Hope and Being Present Work Together

- **Acknowledging Reality:** Being grounded in the present helps you confront your situation honestly, fostering genuine hope based on understanding actual challenges, not wishful thinking.
- **Cultivating Resilience:** Mindfulness nurtures resilience. Hope thrives in this space by finding the strength to face difficulties and keeping hope alive even in tough times.
- **Finding Meaning:** Being present allows you to find purpose in everyday actions. This fuels hope, giving you a reason to keep moving forward and enhancing your vision of a meaningful life.
- **Avoiding Despair:** Staying present helps prevent feeling overwhelmed by past regrets or future anxieties. This balance provides peace, allowing hope to remain steady and strong.

Additional Points:

- **Hope as a Catalyst:** Hope can be a catalyst for action, motivating you to take steps towards your goals and overcome challenges.
- **Present Moment Awareness:** Being present allows you to recognise the small victories and positive moments in your life, which can nourish hope.
- **Avoiding Rumination:** Focusing on the present can help prevent rumination and negative thought patterns that can erode hope.
- **Gratitude Practice:** Cultivating gratitude can strengthen hope by focusing on the positive aspects of your life.
- **Self-Compassion:** Treating yourself with kindness and understanding can boost your resilience and hope.
- **Seeking Support:** Connecting with others who offer support and encouragement can strengthen your hope and sense of belonging.

Tool to Cultivate Hope: The "HOPE" Practice

H	**Hold the Present Moment**	• Mindful Breathing: Sit comfortably and focus on your breath. Notice the sensations of your body and the sounds around you. Let go of past regrets and future worries. • Grounding Exercise: Imagine your roots extending deep into the earth, providing stability and grounding. • Present Moment Awareness: Remind yourself that this moment is the only moment you truly have.
O	**Open to Possibilities**	• Challenge Negative Thoughts: Identify and challenge negative thoughts about the future. Replace them with more positive and hopeful perspectives. • Embrace Uncertainty: Acknowledge that the future is uncertain, but focus on the possibilities rather than the mysteries.
P	**Practice Gratitude**	• Gratitude Journal: Write down three things you are grateful for each day. • Mindful Gratitude: Focus on the present moment and appreciate the small things in your life. • Gratitude Meditation: Visualise yourself surrounded by the things you are grateful for.
E	**Engage in Positive Action**	• Set Small, Achievable Goals: Break down larger goals into smaller, manageable steps. • Celebrate Progress: Acknowledge and celebrate your achievements, no matter how small. Find Meaningful Activities: Engage in activities that bring you joy and fulfilment.

By practising the HOPE technique regularly, you can cultivate a more hopeful mindset.

HOW THE FOUR CARDINAL DIRECTIONS SUPPORT HEALING: INTERCONNECTEDNESS AND SYNERGY

The four cardinal directions of Compassionate Recovery: Response-ability, Acceptance, Forgiveness, and Hope are not isolated concepts. Instead, they function as an interconnected web, with each direction intricately linked. The directions reinforce and complement each other. This interdependence creates a holistic framework for healing and personal growth.

Let's explore how these principles influence and support each other on the journey of recovery:

Response-ability: The Foundation of Empowerment

Response-ability is the foundation upon which the other directions are built. It emphasises taking ownership of your actions and recognising your power to respond to life's challenges with clarity and purpose. Without Response-ability, you may feel powerless to change your circumstances or control your life. By embracing Response-ability, you gain a sense of agency and autonomy, laying the groundwork for personal growth and transformation. It paves the way for acceptance: You can't truly accept a situation without taking ownership of your reactions and choices. Response-ability empowers you to acknowledge your agency and respond effectively, even when faced with challenges. Acceptance then allows you to embrace reality without judgement, creating space for growth.

Acceptance: The Path to Understanding

Acceptance builds upon Response-ability by encouraging you to acknowledge and embrace reality with compassion. It involves accepting both external circumstances and internal experiences without judgement or resistance. Without Response-ability , acceptance becomes challenging, as you may cling to blame or denial. By taking responsibility for your responses, you empower yourself to confront reality with openness and honesty, promoting a deeper sense of acceptance and self-awareness. Acceptance opens the door to forgiveness because accepting yourself and others as human and imperfect helps you let go of blame and resentment. Acceptance creates the understanding and compassion necessary for forgiveness, leading to emotional healing and stronger connections.

Forgiveness: The Key to Healing

Forgiveness is intricately connected to both Response-ability and Acceptance. It involves releasing the burden of the past by letting go of resentment and anger towards oneself and others. Acceptance precedes Forgiveness because, without acceptance, you might resist acknowledging the impact of past experiences or the need for forgiveness. Embracing reality as it is creates fertile ground for forgiveness, enabling you to confront your pain and move toward healing. Similarly, without Responsibility, it is challenging to take ownership of your role in the forgiveness process. By recognising your power to choose your response to past hurts, you can actively engage in forgiveness, freeing yourself from emotional bondage. Forgiveness fuels hope because letting go of past hurts opens the door to new possibilities. Forgiveness allows you to move forward with optimism, believing in a brighter future. Hope sustains forgiveness by motivating you to keep moving forward, even in tough times.

Hope: The Beacon Illuminating the Path

Hope serves as a guiding light that illuminates the path toward healing and wholeness. It instils optimism and resilience, reminding you that positive change is possible even in the face of adversity. Without hope, you may feel discouraged or hopeless about your prospects for recovery and transformation. Hope gives meaning and purpose to the journey, inspiring you to persevere through challenges and setbacks. It also amplifies the impact of forgiveness by motivating you to seek reconciliation and rebuild trust in relationships.

Acceptance Opens the Door to Forgiveness: Accepting yourself and others as human and imperfect helps you let go of blame and resentment. Acceptance creates the understanding and compassion necessary for forgiveness, leading to emotional healing and stronger connections.

Forgiveness Fuels Hope: Letting go of past hurts opens the door to Hope and provides the vision and inspiration to set goals and pursue dreams, which, in turn, fuels Response-ability, the willingness to take action and to make choices to achieve those dreams. Hope keeps you motivated, while responsibility ensures you take concrete steps toward a better future.

These directions create a powerful cycle, each reinforcing the others, leading to greater empowerment, resilience, and well-being. Cultivating these four directions charts a course for a fulfilling life, grounded in your inner strength and ability to navigate life's journey.

RESOURCES

- General Healing and Self-Help

The Four Agreements by Don Miguel Ruiz is a classic self-help book that explores the power of personal transformation through simple agreements with oneself.

The Power of Now by Eckhart Tolle is a spiritual text that emphasises the importance of living in the present moment to overcome suffering and find inner peace.

- Recovery and Addiction

Mindfulness for Beginners by Jon Kabat-Zinn introduces mindfulness meditation as a tool for stress reduction and emotional healing.

The Gifts of Imperfection by Brené Brown explores the importance of vulnerability, shame, resilience, and self-compassion in personal growth and healing.

- Psychology and Therapy

The Courage to Heal by Jean A. Holzworth provides guidance for survivors of childhood sexual abuse, emphasising the importance of healing through understanding, acceptance, and forgiveness.

The Body Keeps the Score by Bessel van der Kolk explores the impact of trauma on the body and mind and offers strategies for healing.

The Mindful Self-Compassion Workbook by Kristin Neff. This workbook provides practical exercises for cultivating self-compassion, which is essential for personal growth and healing.

CONCLUSION

A Revolution of the Heart: A Wayfinder's Journey

Dear fellow traveller,

As our journey draws to a close, let us reflect on the legacy of the Wayfinders, the brave celestial navigators of the Pacific. Their steadfast spirit of exploration, limitless resilience, and deep bond with the stars provide a timeless inspiration, reminding us that the pursuit of discovery depends as much on inner strength as it does on the path ahead.

May our journeys mirror theirs, becoming not merely physical endeavours but profound spiritual quests. May we also bravely face the unknown. Guided by stars, waves, and winds, they carved pathways towards distant horizons, showing us the courage to embrace uncertainty and the wisdom to keep moving forward.

As we continue on our paths of discovery and healing, we draw strength from the example of these ancient mariners. Like them, we must navigate the uncharted waters of addiction - a journey as complex as it is challenging. By exploring and understanding the deep-rooted forces that drive addiction, we can cultivate compassionate and effective approaches to recovery. Just as the Wayfinders relied on shared wisdom and collective experience, so too must we build community and support among those grappling with addiction. By nurturing connection and empathy, we illuminate the path to a brighter future. Together, we can navigate the complexities of addiction, unlock our potential, and embark on a journey of healing and renewal.

Our lives are made up of both happy and challenging moments, including joy, sorrow, triumph and hardship. Each experience and each emotion add texture to the complex landscape of who we are. Within this terrain lies a remarkable, often hidden, capacity for self-creation. We are empowered not only to endure life's highs and lows but to shape our own paths forward, using even the most difficult experiences as stepping stones for growth. We are more than products of our pasts. While our histories shape us, they do not define us. This process of becoming whole calls us to look inward, to integrate our fragmented parts, and to honour both light and shadow within. It reminds us that we are the architects of our futures, capable of transforming pain into purpose and limitations into newfound strengths.

In this journey of self-discovery, we come to see ourselves not as fixed entities but as ever-evolving beings. We realise that our power to redefine ourselves is always within reach. Every choice, every moment of awareness, brings us closer to our true essence, uncovering the unique potential that resides within us. Through courage, introspection, and commitment to growth, we become creators of our lives, shaping meaning and purpose in the vast landscape that lies before us.

We know that self-compassion, empathy, and an unwavering belief in the boundless potential within every person illuminate the path to healing as we continue our exploration. In a world where isolation is all too common, the power of human connection is essential. Every act of kindness, every moment of understanding, ripples outward, inspiring others and cultivating belonging.

The path of compassionate recovery is more than a method – it is a revolution of the heart where we unlock extraordinary potential within ourselves and contribute to a more compassionate world. Let us commit to being catalysts for change, igniting the spark of compassion within and inspiring others to do the same. Let us create a world where kindness, empathy, and understanding prevail and where every person feels valued, connected, and empowered.

I invite you to reflect on what has resonated with you and consider how you might carry these principles forward - whether by offering a listening ear, practising self-compassion, or becoming an advocate for others in their own journeys of healing. Share your story, reach out to others, and build bridges of understanding in your community. Every gesture, no matter how small, can be a spark that ignites hope and change. Let this be a call to create a life that embodies compassion, resilience, and purpose. Together, let's build a world where everyone feels seen, valued, and empowered. You hold the power to be part of this compassionate revolution - one choice, one act, one day at a time. Take this journey with you and make it a lifelong commitment to healing and transformation for yourself and others.

In closing, know that this journey is not one with a final destination but an ongoing, evolving adventure. Each day brings new opportunities to grow, heal, and inspire others as you continue forward. Embrace the journey, trust in your resilience, and let compassion guide your steps. As you navigate your path, remember you are never alone. Fellow travellers walk beside you, each carrying the light of their own experiences, hopes, and dreams. Together, we create a collective strength and a shared purpose that sustains us through the most challenging parts of the journey. Carry forward the wisdom, courage, and compassion you've cultivated. Live each day with purpose, and may your path be filled with moments of clarity, joy, and connection. The world is brighter because of your existence, and the impact you make, however small it may seem, is meaningful beyond measure.

With gratitude and hope,

Vincenzia

Introducing The 12 Stepping Stones: A Practical Path to Healing and Wholeness

As we conclude our journey in From Pain to Purpose, I invite you to continue the journey with my companion book, *The 12 Stepping Stones*. This insightful guide beckons you toward a practical and transformative path of healing and wholeness. Unlike many self-help books that focus on becoming someone new, *The 12 Stepping Stones* encourages you to turn your gaze inward, reconnecting with the essence of who you already are.

This mindful approach is designed to cultivate presence and awareness through the practice of mindfulness. You'll learn to observe yourself with curiosity and kindness, dispelling the tendency toward judgment while paving the way for profound growth. Within these pages, you will also discover mindful attitudes like emotional honesty, patience, humility, and self-compassion.

In a fast-paced world filled with external expectations and societal pressures, it's all too easy to lose touch with your innermost self. Over time, layers of conditioning, fear, trauma, addiction and self-doubt can conceal your inner beauty. By honouring each of the stepping stones, you will learn to anchor yourself in the present moment, cultivating confidence, resilience, and grace amid life's challenges.

The 12 Stepping Stones: A Practical Path to Healing and Wholeness

1. **The First Stepping Stone: Mindfulness**
   Through cultivating present-moment awareness
2. **The Second Stepping Stone: Patience**
   Through nurturing a calm and accepting attitude toward life
3. **The Third Stepping Stone: Impermanence**
   Through embracing change with grace and resilience
4. **The Fourth Stepping Stone: Equanimity**
   Through finding inner peace amidst life's storms

5. **The Fifth Stepping Stone: Humility**
   Through recognising one's limitations and strengths
6. **The Sixth Stepping Stone: Self-Compassion**
   Through cultivating self-love and acceptance
7. **The Seventh Stepping Stone: Emotional Honesty**
   Through embracing authenticity and vulnerability
8. **The Eighth Stepping Stone: Letting Go**
   Through releasing attachments and moving forward
9. **The Ninth Stepping Stone: Witness Consciousness**
   Through observing thoughts and emotions without judgement
10. **The Tenth Stepping Stone: Interconnectedness**
    Through recognising our unity with all beings
11. **The Eleventh Stepping Stone: Trust**
    Through building faith in oneself and the universe
12. **The Twelfth Stepping Stone: Gratitude**
    Through cultivating appreciation for life's blessings

May *The 12 Stepping Stones* serve as a gentle guide, illuminating your path as you navigate your sacred journey toward healing, wholeness, and a deeper connection with your true self.

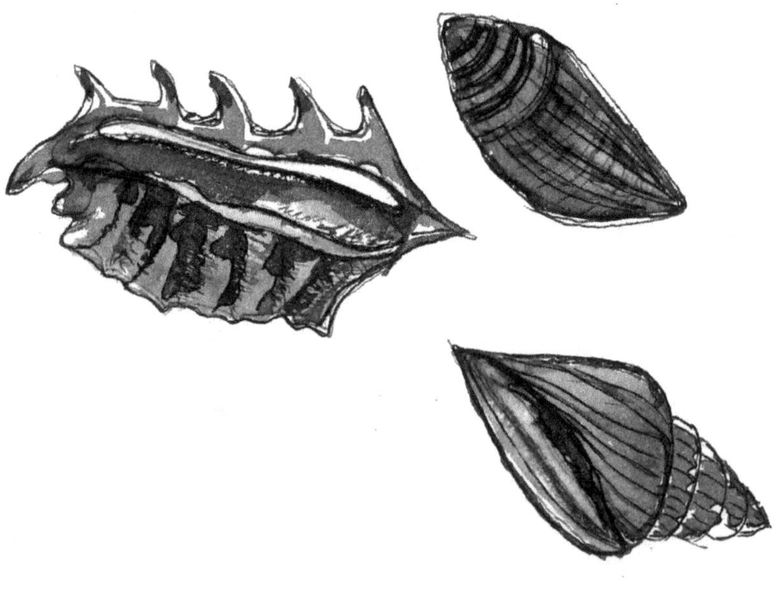

www.ingramcontent.com/pod-product-compliance
Lightning Source LLC
LaVergne TN
LVHW052113210926
848482LV00025B/577

9781037088452